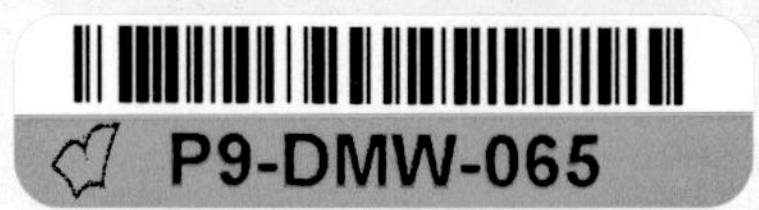

Creating the Peaceable Classroom

Techniques to Calm, Uplift, and Focus Teachers and Students

SANDY BOTHMER

Zephyr Press
Chicago

Creating the Peaceable Classroom:
Techniques to Calm, Uplift, and Focus Teachers and Students

Professional Growth

Printed in the United States of America

ISBN: 1-56976-154-X

Editing: Kirsteen E. Anderson
Design and Production: Dan Miedaner
Illustrations: Jan Sattler
Photographs: Brian Woodbury
Cover: Dan Miedaner

Published by:
Zephyr Press
An imprint of Chicago Review Press
814 North Franklin Street
Chicago, Illinois 60610
(800) 232-2187
www.zephyrpress.com

Library of Congress Cataloging-in-Publication Data

Bothmer, Sandy, 1947-
Creating the peaceable classroom : techniques to calm, uplift, and focus teachers and students / Sandy Bothmer.
p. cm.
Includes bibliographical references (p.) and index.
ISBN 1-56976-154-X
1. Classroom environment. 2. Teaching—Psychological aspects. 3. Stress management. 4. Exercise therapy. I. Title.
LB3013 .B63 2003
371.102'4—dc21

2002013850

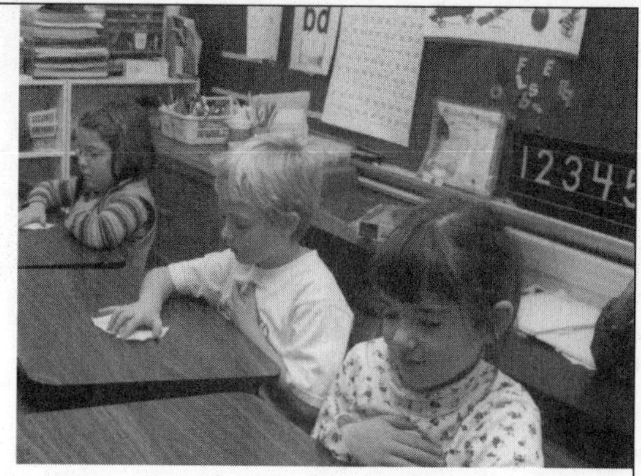

Creating the Peaceable Classroom

Techniques to Calm, Uplift, and Focus Teachers and Students

Sandy Bothmer

Dedication

This book is dedicated to teachers and their students in the happy hope that they will run and play with these ideas and make them their own.

Acknowledgments

A book is made not by one, but with the help of many. I wish to express my gratitude to the many who have helped me on this project. Heartfelt thanks to all!

- To the Zephyr Press staff for believing in this project. Special thanks go to my editors, Jenny Flynn, who saw the promise of a book in a University of Connecticut Confratute conference flyer; and Ronnie Durie, for gently guiding me through the process. Thanks also go to Dan Miedaner, art director, for the fluid, unified layout and design of this book.
- To Kirsteen Anderson for carefully refining the text.
- To Richard Bothmer, my husband and greatest supporter and sounding board, who encouraged me from the start to "go for it!" reminding me that publishing a book has been my lifetime dream.
- To Jan Sattler, my artist, for her deep belief in this project and her creative expression of the text.
- To Brian Woodbury, my photographer, whose photographs have captured the essence of the feng shui elements and the goodness of childhood in the faces of the children he has photographed.
- To my feng shui consultant, Laurie Biggers, for consulting with me on part 1, sharing her expertise, and helping me find a concise and teacher-friendly way to present this ancient Chinese practice.
- To Stephanie Rutt, my yoga teacher, for her consultation on breathing techniques and for all she has taught me about the importance of the breath and living each moment from the heart.
- To Patsy Brightman, Rosemary Todd Clough, Ginny Jackson, and Marina Walker, my yoga teacher friends, for consulting with me on the yoga and breathing sections in this book.
- To Fritz Bell and Rosemary Todd Clough, my movement teachers, who in their individual ways have taught me the importance of movement in the learning process.
- To Superintendent Ken DeBenedictis, Supervising Principal Eileen Fucile, and Associate Principals Carol Thibaudeau and Ann Windsor, for their support of this project and permission to work with the teachers and students in the Hollis, New Hampshire, elementary schools.
- To Brenda Arel, Lee Barnard, Sue Connelly, Brenda Golia, Phyllis Gray, Lindy Hanninen, Ellen Lencsak, Sue Manigan, Roisin McElroy, Mary Lou Noonan, Cheryl Paradis, Linda Pellerin, Carol Smiglin, Mary Ann Smith, and Amy Ziminsky, Hollis Primary School or Hollis Upper Elementary School staff members, former colleagues, and friends, who shared their students or classrooms with me.
- All of the parents who gave me permission to photograph their children. These photographs make the text come alive!

Contents

Introduction

The rewards of teaching are many, but for me there was nothing more rewarding than nurturing and supporting my students' growth. Watching their skills and understanding grow and blossom was truly a gift. Those "Ah ha! I get it!" moments were wonderful! But each year, I found it increasingly more difficult to meet my students' emotional and learning needs, and from what I hear and see, teaching is no easier now than when I was in the trenches. Perhaps it's even more difficult.

Many teachers are overwhelmed with greater and greater amounts of curriculum to cover without being able to let go of anything to make room for the new. Professional and community expectations seem to be increasing, and our personal lives may present their own challenges. A son does not plan to get the flu around your report card deadline. Nor does an aging mother plan a stroke around your work week. Even if your administrators are supportive, all these factors create a burden of stress. At times, stress in one of its many guises may make it difficult to be fully present at school, to be "on," so to speak, in a job that requires it. Does this sound familiar?

> The best teachers will know how to influence learners' states and moods; and how to better manage their own feelings.
>
> —Eric Jensen
> *Super Teaching* (p. 26)

And what about your students? Even they are affected by the whirlwind of life. Family concerns, scholastic and parental expectations, competition, friendships, and outside activities have an impact on their lives, no matter how young they are. Focusing on academics may be extremely difficult for a youngster when thoughts of a grandfather in the hospital keep intruding or images of the family's sick cat keep popping up. Then there is the argument with a best friend on the playground that dogs the student after recess. These are just a few of the many scenarios that may cause students to feel distracted, uneasy, and unable to focus on doing their best work in the classroom.

Creating the Peaceable Classroom offers techniques that will help you create a nurturing and supportive classroom environment where optimum teaching and learning can take place. It also offers you, the teacher, strategies for moving through emotions or distractions that may interfere with your ability to be focused and fully present as you work with your students. In addition, I offer similar techniques in the form of lessons you can use with your students to help them move through their emotions and distractions as well. I do not mean to imply that it is not important to resolve problems. Indeed it is, and in some cases, they need to be dealt with immediately. In many cases, though, the problems cannot be resolved quickly, and the classroom is not the best place to address them. More appropriate contexts would be in private with you or the school counselor (for example, think of a student whose parents are divorcing). In such cases, the best we can do for ourselves and our students is to "put the distractions on the shelf," as my yoga teacher often says, so everyone can function better at school. We can take the issues off the shelf when the lesson or the day is over and look at them in a better time and place.

By enhancing the nurturing and supportive environment of your classroom, you can make it as stress free as possible. No one can eliminate the stressors that you and your students walk in the door with, but you can create a setting conducive to optimum teaching and learning, transforming the stress you and your students hold. With a calming environment, you and your students can use techniques proactively to further the release of stress and emotions.

So imagine yourself at a Chinese restaurant ordering a pu pu platter. It comes to you sizzling hot with a number of dishes for you to sample. Choose one dish, one technique, and bite into it. Chew it a bit. Savor it. Decide if you like it. Some of the dishes, or techniques, you'll like better than others. That's all right. Once you've sampled everything on the platter, you'll know what appeals to you, what nourishes you, and you can order more next time. Experiment with these techniques to find out how they work best for you and your students, either individually or collectively. They will go a long way in supporting your creation of a peaceable classroom where you and your students can do your best work!

The brain stays alert and relaxed for learning in a safe and positive learning environment.

—Eric Jensen
Super Teaching (p. 26)

What's Inside

This book is divided into three parts, addressing the classroom space, the teacher, and the student, respectively. In Part I, I offer you techniques to maximize the nurturing and supportive environment within your classroom. You will discover how the ancient Chinese practice of feng shui—with its three tenets of connectedness, balance, and vitality and five elements of fire, earth, metal, water, and wood—can provide simple, commonsense guidance in enhancing the learning spaces already present in your classroom. Creating a peaceable classroom is all a matter of assessing what is already present and then making adjustments according to the fluctuating needs of your students. For thousands of years, the people of China have brought peace and harmony into their homes through these practices, and now you can realize the same benefits in your classroom as well.

Part II is for you, the teacher. In it I introduce you to techniques that will help you relax or energize your body. I explain and discuss breathing patterns, meditation, yoga postures (some modified to fit the classroom setting), *Reiki* (a Japanese natural healing practice), and movement experiences to help you release emotions and distractions that make it difficult for you to be fully present, to focus, and to do your best work each day. You can use these techniques at home if you wish and at school when needed.

Part III, the student section, can help you tune in to the emotional temperature of your students so you can help them individually or collectively change their state of being, allowing them to focus and do their best work. Breathing patterns, centering activities, yoga postures, movement experiences, and different types of music are strategies you can use to help your students feel more relaxed or energized. Use them during transition times, as pick-me-uppers when lethargy appears, or during your class meeting time. You, too, will benefit as you guide your students in these techniques.

Using this Book

How should you go about using this book? I would suggest you read through the chapters in order, because they are organized upon a continuum of desired effects. In Part I, you focus on creating a comfortable and inviting, nurturing and supportive classroom environment where optimum teaching and learning can take place. In Part II, you look at how you can remain in a good state of being within that space, fully focused and able to give your best to your teaching efforts. Part III provides you with lessons and activities that will assist your students in maintaining or regaining their focus so that they, too, can do their best work. My hope is that you and your students will internalize some of these techniques and transfer them to many aspects of your daily living, for they are just plain "good medicine" for living a peaceable, balanced life.

Slow, deep breathing is probably the single best anti-stress medicine we have.

—James Gordon
Clinical Professor of Psychiatry
Georgetown University School of Medicine

Since there is some crossover between Parts II and III, the techniques for the teacher and those for students, you might find it helpful to introduce a technique with your students as you are learning it yourself. Deep abdominal breathing and yoga postures are techniques that lend themselves to this format.

When introducing your students to a technique, you will want to explain what it will do for them—how it will assist them in relaxing or energizing so they can do their best work. (For example, "Today, we are going to learn a breathing technique that will help us to relax and calm down.") Later, when you suggest that they use a technique during the course of a day, remind them of its purpose.

(For example, "I can see that some of you are nervous about this test. Let's all do some deep abdominal breathing so we can feel calmer. Sit up straight. Breathe in. . . .")

You might introduce these techniques during your class meeting time, when a "teachable moment" arises, or during a transition time. Eventually, having a menu of techniques for your students to choose from will empower each student to use the technique that works best for him or her. Some students may spontaneously begin to use different techniques for different situations.

As you read, you will notice questions with a ✎ next to them. This icon suggests that you pause to write your thoughts or observations about the questions in a journal. You may want to refer to your journal from time to time as you reassess your classroom environment.

Why Should I Use These Techniques?

Now, if you are as busy a teacher as I was, you are probably asking yourself, "How can I spend time on these techniques when I have so little teaching time to begin with?" Let me assure you that most of these strategies take only a few minutes once your students know how to do them. Certain activities you might need to spend more time on, and others you might choose to spend more time on, depending on your and your students' needs. The little extra time you spend will go a long way in improving your students' abilities to focus on their work. Using these techniques, they are likely to accomplish more work in less time, and to do better-quality work. So check off the time element as a non-issue!

Benefits

The strategies I offer in *Creating the Peaceable Classroom*

- require minimal time investment
- improve well-being
- improve attention and focus
- increase teaching success
- increase learning success

Those of you feeling pressured to improve test scores and student performance are probably thinking, "Feeling good is nice, but what about academic success? Will these techniques help my students

> I see greater confidence and more relaxation in my students as they approach and go through the state testing process. I attribute this in part to their use of deep abdominal breathing and affirmations. Many of my students do better as well.
>
> —Third-grade teacher

where it really counts?" The short answer is yes. Now, here's the long answer. According to Principal Zane Cantrell, who implemented a program called "The Breathe System" at Black Fox Elementary School in Murfreesboro, Tennessee, relaxation techniques resulted in improved test scores and fewer arguments between students ("Technique" 2001). Finger-walking along a spiral is another strategy that helps some students improve their test scores. One fourth grader I worked with was regularly scoring 40 or 50 percent on math quizzes and tests. Once he started finger-walking a spiral before starting the test, his scores improved into the 80 percent range, simply because he was more relaxed and could focus on test taking. Physician James Gordon, a clinical professor of psychiatry at Georgetown University School of Medicine and director of the Center for Mind-Body Medicine in the District of Columbia, teaches deep abdominal breathing to most of his patients, including children who have been diagnosed with attention deficit disorder. He reports that deep breathing helps to reduce anxiety and calm the mind (Krucoff 2000, 11). Undoubtedly, students who are less anxious are better able to focus their mental resources on their schoolwork, a necessary condition for better performance. These strategies will benefit all students, but because they produce a calm, focused state of heightened attention, they may particularly benefit students who have attention deficit disorder or test-taking anxiety.

By adopting these techniques, you will enhance your own well-being and teaching success. Given the high rate of burnout among teachers, you deserve to take the best possible care of yourself. At the same time, you will improve your students' well-being and learning success. You will launch your students on a life path of self-empowerment, for as they internalize these techniques and make them a part of their daily lives, they will grow into adults who are well equipped to face the challenges and stressors in their lives. What a gift you will have given them!

And you will give the parents of your students a gift as well, as they see their children handle emotional ups and downs better and function better in school. In fact, not long ago I spoke to the mother of one of my former third graders, who is now a sophomore in high school. She said that the centering techniques her son learned in my classroom have stayed with him, becoming a part of his self-care kit. This is what *Creating the Peaceable Classroom* is all about.

I have never had a parent take issue with the relaxation and energizing techniques I have taught their children. In the unlikely event a parent expresses concern to you, I suggest you simply explain how and why these techniques are beneficial. You might invite the parent into your classroom to observe the strategies in action or, perhaps, to participate in them during a class meeting. Seeing and doing is believing. Such a visit will reassure the parent that these techniques are, indeed, worthy of learning.

Now, it's time to sample the pu pu platter of strategies for a peaceable classroom.

Part I

Optimizing the Classroom Environment

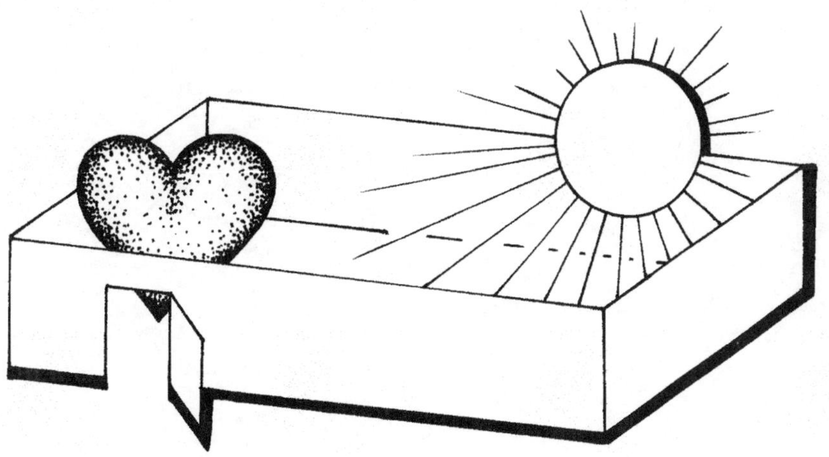

Creating a nurturing and supportive classroom environment comes from the heart: love for yourself, love for your students, and love for teaching and learning. Looking at the environment is the first step toward creating a peaceable classroom. Begin by asking yourself these questions:

 *What can I do to create an environment that will make me feel good and assist me in doing my best work?*

 *What can I do to create an environment that will make my students feel good and assist them in doing their best work?*

The answers to these questions hold the keys to effective teaching and learning. Guidance in answering them can be found in the practice of feng shui.

Chapter 1

Feng Shui? Feng What?

***Feng shui** (pronounced* fung shway*) is an ancient Chinese practice derived from the awareness that the elements of the natural world affect our being. We are affected by the caress of the breeze, the sun shining on our faces, and the plants in our yards. Because most of us spend the majority of our time indoors, we are not as closely connected to the earth or as stimulated by the rhythms of the outdoor elements as we once were. Feng shui symbolically brings the outdoors inside, allowing you and your students to experience the elements daily. A nurturing and supportive environment is the result. Through feng shui, your classroom becomes a place where good things happen!*

Nancilee Wydra, feng shui consultant and author of *Feng Shui: The Book of Cures,* writes, "Interaction with the world is impaired when our surroundings are not nourishing" (Wydra 1996, 13). Relating this statement to the classroom, teaching and learning interactions are impaired if the environment is not nourishing. The three feng shui tenets of connectedness, balance, and vitality offer guides for making adjustments in your classroom that promote a nourishing environment for you and your students.

The first tenet of feng shui, **connectedness,** relates to feeling connected to the natural world, your ancestors and family, the universe, and even role models who have inspired you (for example, Nelson Mandela or Mother Teresa). It is important for you and your students to feel connected to the classroom space and one another. Certainly, displaying your students' work in the classroom and outside in the hallway promotes connection (as well as sending a message that you value academic accomplishments). Framing your class photo and hanging it in a prominent position, perhaps outside the door for all to see as they enter, makes a positive statement, "We live here!" As you and your students enter the classroom each day, you see that message of belonging and connectedness.

In what ways do you promote connectedness in your classroom?

Balance in a space is evaluated by its **yin** (quiet) and **yang** (active) aspects. By its nature a classroom has both yin and yang features. That is, both types of activities take place there. The space needs to be stimulating but not overly stimulating; relaxing but not overly relaxing. You don't want your students constantly being noisy, nor do you want them nodding off. Balance is the key.

In what ways do you bring balance into your classroom?

Vitality can be described as aliveness. It is the force that turns a seed into a plant, a single cell into an embryo. Have you ever walked into a room and immediately felt uplifted, at ease, comfortable? In contrast, have you ever walked into a room and felt heavy, uneasy, uncomfortable? These reactions are a result of the aliveness, or vitality, of the room in the former case, and the lack thereof in the latter. Vitality has both a physical and emotional impact. If the vitality of your classroom is uplifting, everyone can do their best work.

What is the vitality of your classroom like?

Does the vitality of your classroom change? If so, when?

Connectedness, balance, and vitality are established through the presence of five elements: fire, earth, metal, water, and wood. Used together, in varying degrees, these elements promote harmony in your classroom by symbolically bringing the natural world inside.

The Five Elements

To help people understand the five elements, feng shui consultant Laurie Biggers, of Amherst, New Hampshire, associates each one with a word that represents how it influences the classroom environment. As you plan your classroom space, consider the effects of each element and how you can balance them in each area of your room to create a space conducive to the kinds of activities that take place there.

fire = action: The classroom environment needs to have an age-appropriate level of stimulation to focus activity for learning.

earth = support: The classroom environment needs to be safe and supportive.

metal = containment: The classroom environment needs to have some boundaries, or containment, so there is a feeling of being in control and everyone is able to focus.

water = flexibility: The classroom environment needs to be flexible to allow for changes when needed.

wood = growth: The classroom environment needs to promote growth in you and your students.

Incorporating the Five Elements into Your Classroom

So, how do you incorporate these feng shui elements in your classroom in the right amounts to achieve this important balance? Let's examine the five elements individually and how you might use each to promote a nurturing and supportive classroom environment. I will suggest specific adjustments, all of which you can make with little or no outside help.

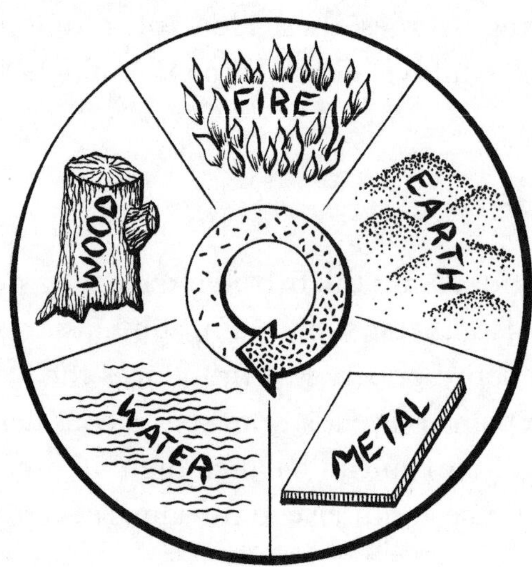

Fire Adjustments

The fire element promotes and represents action. Certainly, a classroom is a place of action, but you don't want the activity to flare out of control. Thoughtful selection of appropriate feng shui elements can achieve this balance.

Symbols of the element fire include the color red, electricity, movement, and triangular shapes. You almost certainly already have the fire element present in your classroom. Electrical wiring, air vents, lights, tape recorders, and computers are all expressions of fire. Here are a few other ways that you can incorporate this element in areas of your classroom where you want greater stimulation. Use these suggestions judiciously, as overuse may hinder your students' learning.

Charts

Use red paper to mount or create charts of important information that you want your students to remember or refer to regularly. Any shade of red will do: fire engine red, brick red, orange red, and so on. My personal preference is a pure, primary red because it definitely attracts the eye. In his book *Super Teaching,* Eric Jensen recommends that information you want your students to review regularly is best placed above eye level, because this placement stimulates the recall of information through the visual mode. He adds that charts have more impact on students' memories when you place them on the side walls rather than at the front of the room (Jensen 1995).

Objects to Create Movement

To add a sense of movement in your classroom, hang a wind chime by a window or near an air vent. The air flow will cause the chime to sound, adding stimulation to the environment. The tinkling may even arouse a few drowsy students! A wind chime is also a pleasant way to signal your students when their attention is needed. If you wish to use the chime in this way, be sure to hang it in a place where you spend a good bit of your time, perhaps in the front of the room near the chalkboard.

Another way to create movement is to place a small fan behind a green plant. The moving air will create a gentle rustling of leaves. Of course, opening the windows will also do the trick whenever you want to enhance the vitality of the room.

Classroom Pets

If your school policy allows this, bring a furry pet into your classroom to increase the sense of action. Caring for the animal is also a great way to encourage responsibility in your students. Before adopting a classroom pet, it is wise to notify parents and ensure that none of the students have allergies or asthma that might be triggered by animal fur.

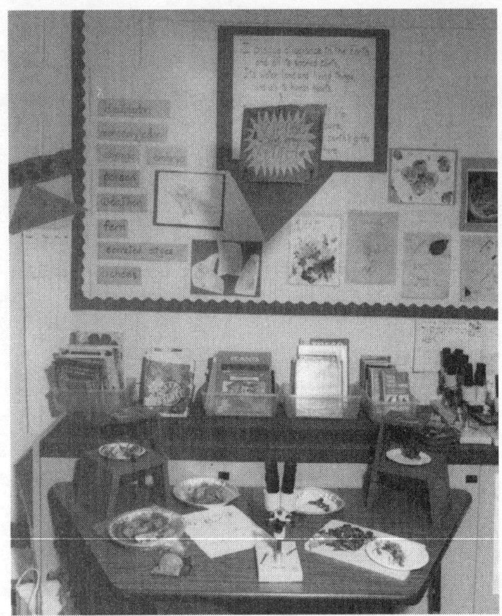

Mounting this science center sign on a red paper triangle introduces a touch of the fire element to the classroom.

Triangular Signs

Use hanging red triangles to label areas where active individual or paired learning experiences take place, such as a science learning center on seeds or magnets. For younger students, the shape of the sign offers another opportunity to review geometric shapes.

 *How does the fire element appear in your classroom?*

 *Is there too much or too little of the fire element in your classroom? If so, what adjustments can you make to improve the balance of this element?*

Earth Adjustments

The earth element promotes and represents support. Like the earth, which generates gravity and keeps you connected to it, so too, must the classroom provide a sense of support and connection. The earth element is also related to the heart, the center of your vitality. Just like a person, your classroom needs a heart, a center from which your students' learning emanates. Using earth adjustments will help you create a supportive environment of belonging and connectedness.

Symbols of the element earth include the colors yellow, terra cotta, and brown or other earth tones; squares and cubes; feelings of safety, security, and peace; and the heart. You already have tables or desks and chairs in your classroom, and probably at least one square computer screen, all expressions of the earth element. Here are some other ways to enhance this element in your classroom.

Sofas

Bring a sofa into your classroom, perhaps in your reading corner, as a place for your students to snuggle up and read during free time or silent reading time. The sofa provides a safe, supportive place to spend time. If possible, choose a sofa upholstered in an earth color or cover it with an earth-toned slip cover or lengths of fabric sewn together.

Square Throw Pillows

Adding square throw pillows in your reading corner or on a sofa promotes a sense of safety and security. Again, try to choose earth element colors.

Bringing in an earth-toned sofa with square pillows helps to create a safe, supportive reading area in this classroom.

Rugs

Place a special rug in your reading corner or classroom meeting area. The rug defines the space where you and your students gather, as well as promoting a feeling of safety.

Small Square Tables

Use a small square table in your reading corner to showcase selected books or as a place for a plant, fountain, or small lamp.

 *How does the earth element appear in your classroom?*

 *Is there too much or too little of the earth element in your classroom? If so, what adjustments can you make to improve the balance of this element?*

Metal Adjustments

The element metal promotes and represents containment. Your classroom needs containment to provide a sense of order and boundaries. Most likely, your classroom already has chairs, desks, and work tables with metal legs. You probably also have a boom box or radio, a computer, and if you're lucky, a telephone in your classroom. With these items containing metal attributes, you have a start at promoting containment in your classroom without any effort at all. Symbols for the metal element include the colors white and steel gray, as well as metallic or reflective hues such as copper, gold, and silver. Round shapes are also metal symbols.

Round Tables

Round work tables bring in the metal element while promoting a sense of equality among those gathered at them, because there is no head to the table. Another benefit is that a round table creates a curved pathway in the room, slowing down and softening the flow of energy around it.

The metal lamps in this reading corner add a sense of containment to the classroom space and create a quiet setting for read-aloud sessions.

Lamps

Place a metal lamp on your desk or in the reading corner to be turned on during a read-aloud session. If possible, use a full-spectrum light bulb that replicates the wavelengths of natural sunlight. You and your students alike will appreciate a break from the glare of fluorescent lighting (Frey 1999).

How does the metal element appear in your classroom?

Is there too much or too little of the metal element in your classroom? If so, what adjustments can you make to improve the balance of this element?

Water Adjustments

The water element promotes and represents flexibility. In the natural world, water is yielding. If a stream of water encounters a boulder, it will flow around it. So, too, must your classroom be flexible and yielding, allowing for changes of direction.

Symbols of the water element include black and other dark colors, glass, and wavy shapes. If your classroom has a sink and faucet in it, or glass windows, you are already on your way to balancing the water element. Here are other possible water adjustments.

Fish Tank

A soothing way to bring the water element into your classroom is with a fish tank. Your students will enjoy watching the fish and can learn responsibility through caring for them as well.

Fountain

A fountain is a calming addition to any classroom. The soft trickling of a fountain is reminiscent of the peace and calm that comes from listening to a gently flowing stream. You might place a fountain in your class meeting area and use it from time to time as the focus of a centering activity (see chapter 11).

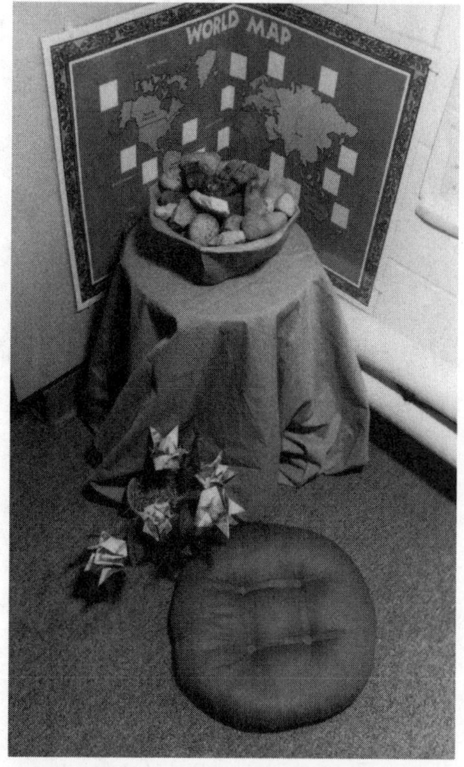

The soft trickle of a water fountain promotes a feeling of peace and calm in this classroom.

Wheeled Cart

A cart on wheels provides a handy place to store small manipulatives or art materials such as containers of markers, crayons, colored pencils, construction paper, glue sticks, or yarn. In seconds, you can pull out the cart and roll it wherever it is needed. A cart also is useful as a mini desk. Put your plan book, school forms, pencils, markers, labels, and other supplies you regularly use on it. Position it in the front of the room or wherever you spend most of your time, and wheel it with you to other parts of the room as needed.

Fabric with a Wavy Pattern

Hang valences with a wavy pattern at your windows.

How does the water element appear in your classroom?

Is there too much or too little of the water element in your classroom? If so, what adjustments can you make to improve the balance of this element?

Wood Adjustments

The element of wood promotes and represents growth. Certainly the ultimate goal for your students is growth: growth in academic skills, thinking skills, creativity, emotional skills, and social skills. Nurturing growth is what teaching and learning are all about!

Symbols of the element wood include the color green, tall and rectangular objects, wooden objects, and the experience of growth. Fortunately, the nature of a classroom automatically provides for elements of wood. There are wooden pencils, magazines, and perhaps newspapers. You may even have wooden desks, tables, or bookshelves. Your windows may be framed in wood. If the wood element is sparse in your classroom, here are some easy ways to intensify it.

This teacher introduced the wood element into her classroom with a wooden computer station, which she personalized by adding some family pictures framed in wood.

Wooden Picture Frames

Display prints, photos, or other artwork in wooden frames. For example, you might hang a reproduction of a famous work of art. Not only does this bring in the wood element, but it offers an opportunity to learn about the work of a master artist. Another idea is to bring in framed family photos to display on your desk. This helps to personalize your space and brings your personal connections into the classroom. Your students might each bring in one special photo framed in wood to place on his or her desk or table. These photos may comfort students during difficult times.

Tree Branch

Create a classroom display piece by hanging a branch from the ceiling or cementing one in a coffee can. Use it to hang seasonal artwork or poetry. You might create a Poetry Tree by having your students write poems on construction-paper leaves that they attach to the branches. Add to the seasonal theme by using green leaves in springtime; orange, red, and yellow ones in fall; and snowflakes for winter.

Plants

Lush green plants add vitality to a classroom as well as being aesthetically pleasing. They are especially welcome if you live in northern climes with long winter months of snow. Plants have an added benefit of removing carbon dioxide and purifying the air. Golden pothos, areca palm, and dracena are recommended for overall air purification. Boston fern and English ivy are among the best plants for eliminating formaldehyde, a common indoor toxin (Lusk 1998). In addition to these benefits, your students have another opportunity to take on responsibilities through plant care.

The lush green of these hanging plants adds vitality to the classroom.

How does the wood element appear in your classroom?

Is there too much or too little of the wood element in your classroom? If so, what adjustments can you make to improve the balance of this element?

As you can see, adding the five feng shui elements to your classroom is not very difficult. In most cases, the elements are already there to some degree, so you don't have to start from scratch. Your careful observation and analysis of the classroom space and your students will tell you if you need more or less of a particular element. If you should be the lucky recipient of new room furnishings, keep the five elements—fire, earth, metal, water, and wood—in mind as you make your choices. Use the adjustments I suggest as a starting point to find your own personalized ways to add the elements. Not only the balance of the five elements, but also the room arrangement contribute to a peaceable environment. Suggestions for arranging your room will be the topic of chapter 2.

Chapter 2

Bringing Balance and Vitality to the Classroom Arrangement

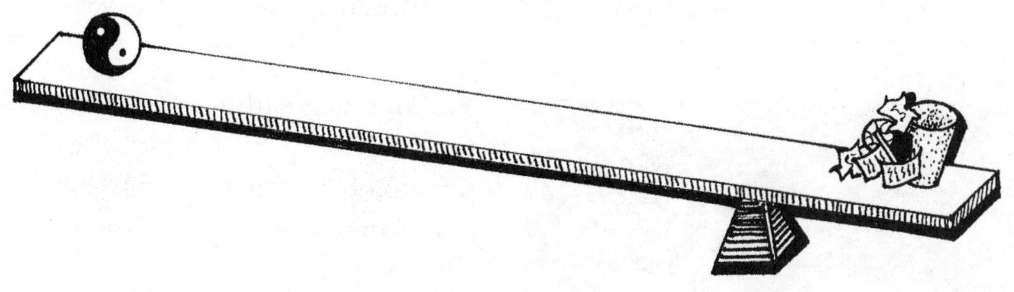

Another aspect of feng shui involves evaluating the classroom space. As a place of learning, the classroom is used for both quiet (yin) and active (yang) experiences. It is important to consider what these experiences are when arranging your classroom space, so you create balanced spaces. Here are some examples of both types of experiences in a classroom:

Yin (quiet): centering, silent reading, testing, independent work, teacher read-alouds

Yang (active): large-group activities (such as a classroom meeting), movement activities, games, small-group activities (such as cooperative learning groups, book buddies, or partnered activities)

What are some of the yin experiences my students will have this year?

What are some of the yang experiences my students will have this year?

The energy connected to these experiences will be either yin or yang as well. For example, independent, silent reading will have cool, calming energy, whereas a whole-class movement activity will have warm, active energy. Sometimes both quiet and active experiences will occur within the same activity. A classroom meeting may begin actively with singing songs and then end quietly with a centering activity to help your students refocus before a lesson begins.

Now that you are aware of the yin and yang experiences of your classroom, consider the creation of yin and yang spaces for these activities. Here are some examples of classroom spaces:

The reading area in this classroom doubles as a classroom meeting space, thus serving both yin and yang purposes at different times.

Yin spaces: reading area, computer area (for individual use), private work area, individual students' desk space

Yang spaces: classroom meeting area, desk space (when groups of students work collaboratively), computer area (if pairs of students work together), learning centers

What types of yin spaces will my students need?

What types of yang spaces will my students need?

It may be that an area will need to double as both a yin and a yang space. For example, your classroom meeting space may also serve as a reading space, game space, or performing space. If furniture needs to be moved in such a case, it is important that your students learn to do this safely and quickly. Their input, along with experimentation and practice, can minimize transition time.

Once you have considered the types of spaces you will need, it's time to do some serious furniture placement.

Arranging the Furniture and Spaces with Vitality in Mind

Thoughtful arrangement of the furniture in your classroom can create optimum vitality, or aliveness. You can promote vitality by making clear pathways between desks and other furniture so energy (and young bodies) can flow easily. When planning your arrangement, consider the following questions:

- Where is the best place for my desk?
- What are the individual needs of my students?
- How can I arrange the furniture to meet these needs?
- What needs are connected to the experiences my students will have in each space?
- How can I best arrange the furniture to meet these needs?
- Where will the yin (quiet) and yang (active) spaces be?
- Where can I create private work spaces for students who are easily distracted?
- Where will the major pathways be?
- Are the pathways safe?
- Where will I store classroom and teacher materials?
- Where will my students store their materials?

Desk Arrangements

Because you are in charge in your classroom, first consider where your desk will be. According to the principles of feng shui, your desk needs to be in a power position, one where you are able to see the main entrance to your classroom. The most common power position is in the farthest corner from the main doorway. If you have other doors, don't worry about them. It is the main entrance, the entrance where your students and visitors enter, that matters.

Typically, the chalkboards or whiteboards in your classroom will dictate the direction that students' desks face. In determining how to arrange the desks, consider the individual needs of your students and the types of activities you will be doing:

- Do you have students with attention issues, behavioral issues, or personal aides?
- Will you be doing a lot of collaborative or small-group work?
- If so, do you have work tables where groups can go to meet, or will students' desks double for this purpose?
- If your students' desks will be used for collaborative work, can they be rearranged quickly and easily, or is it best to arrange them in clusters?

This cluster arrangement facilitates collaborative work, as the small table in the center provides extra work space for each group.

Arranging Other Spaces

Once you have arranged your desk and the core learning space, you can decide where to create an open space for a reading corner and class meeting area. Next, decide where your computer area will be. Consider your expectations for this area: Is the computer space primarily a yin space where students work independently, or is it a yang space where students work as partners? Perhaps it is both, in which case, you will want to think about where to locate it in relation to your reading area and the core learning space.

Also consider where you will have private work spaces and a time-out space. Certainly, both need to be near relatively quiet work areas and away from the major traffic pathways. For example, a private work space near the main doorway would not be conducive to learning. If an electrical outlet is needed in a private work space, make sure to allow for this. The time-out area needs to be somewhat separate from the core learning and gathering spaces but within your constant view. Students who spend time here also need to be able to slip back unobtrusively to their groups or seats when they have calmed down or are more focused.

Set up to the side of the core learning area, this computer/reading space is shielded from distractions by latticed screens.

Other spaces you may wish to create are student mailboxes, learning centers, and puzzle tables. More than likely, the spaces or centers will change from time to time. Just keep in mind that yin (quiet) activities need to be near other yin spaces and yang (active) activities need to be near other yang spaces. Another option is for a choice of yin activities to be happening simultaneously or a choice of yang activities to be happening simultaneously. Under such a system, a work table may be the site of both yin and yang activities as the need arises.

Classroom Vitality

As you will recall, **vitality** in feng shui relates to the aliveness of the space. So it is important that you check for aliveness—the ability of energy to flow easily—in your classroom. Examining the pathways in your classroom is a good place to start. Take a good look at your space and ask yourself the following questions:

- Is there more than one pathway from the main entrance to the core learning area in the classroom?
- Is there enough space for students to pass easily and safely in these pathways?

The vitality of your classroom is also influenced by the amount of "stuff" that lives in your space, including extra furniture, items that adorn your classroom, and teacher and student materials. When too much learning paraphernalia is piled up, overflowing its intended storage shelves, or too many work tables make for narrow, unsafe pathways, the energy flow in your classroom slows down and collects, becoming stagnant. This is not what you want. Nor do you want the safety hazard that too much stuff creates.

Clear pathways and absence of clutter allow easy movement of energy (and bodies) in this classroom.

When you are examining your classroom for vitality, keep in mind that less is best unless you have a good way to store the material or it has dual or multiple purposes. One year, I had to remove a couple of work tables because, as one student put it on the first day of school, "We're like sardines in here!" She was right. I could hardly stand the environment myself. Moving around the room was next to impossible. No one and no space was sacred. I removed some furniture, and the second day of school found us all more relaxed, because we all had more personal space and room to move without bumping into someone or the furniture.

Clutter is another factor that reduces the vitality in your classroom. From a feng shui perspective, clutter is a definite no no! Clutter causes the energy in a space to become trapped and stagnant. This stagnant energy depletes the energy of those in the space, making it more difficult to think clearly and get to work. Therefore, finding a good way to store both frequently used and infrequently used materials is essential. Keeping materials orderly during an activity is just as important as having a place to put them when you're done. For many of us, this aspect of teaching is a nightmare. Often we get so involved in teaching that the straightening, putting-away piece is lost. Not good!

So, what do you do? Answering these questions will help you find solutions:

- What materials do my students use frequently? Where can these materials be put for easy access?
- Are there materials that are outdated or haven't been used in a couple of years? Do I need to keep hanging on to them?
- Do I have enough storage space?
- Could I store my materials in a better way?
- Is there a better way to handle refiling or putting away my materials?
- Is there a better way or place to put student work and work folders?
- Can a student be placed in charge of straightening work areas during use?
- Are my students' personal storage areas adequate?

Putting rarely used materials out to pasture is extremely painful for most teachers. I have often said to myself, "But I just might need it!" even though I haven't touched the material, nor have my students touched it, for years. The fact of the matter is, if you haven't used something in two years or so, you probably aren't ever going to use it! Put these materials on a give-away table in your teacher's lounge for someone else to use. Chances are another teacher *will* use them because they are new to him or her and that class. Another option would be to donate the materials to a local charity. If nothing else, find a spot for them in your attic or garage until you can bear to part with them.

Storage is always an issue. Is there ever enough? Part of the storage solution lies in having enough shelving. If your classroom is lacking, try to get more shelving through your yearly budget, or see if any parents might be able to build you some. If you still don't have enough storage space, you may need to do as I did and store some of your materials at home.

Use of plastic storage containers reduces clutter, thus increasing the vitality of the classroom space.

Having shelves is not enough; some things need to be stored inside containers. Putting materials into durable, plastic containers or heavy-duty cardboard boxes that can be housed easily on shelves or stacked safely against a wall works well.

From a feng shui point of view, it is best not to store things under your desk or tables whenever possible, as this is a place where energy can collect and reduce the vitality in your classroom. This has ill effects, just as clutter does.

Storing your students' materials is also an important consideration. Certainly some materials can be stored in their desks, but what about various work folders and folders of completed work to go home? These need a place too. A set of crates with hanging file folders, one folder for each student, is an option. You might also use a different colored portfolio for each subject, one per student, and house them in plastic or cardboard file boxes or crates. Dividing the folders or files among two or three crates will decrease congestion when students retrieve them.

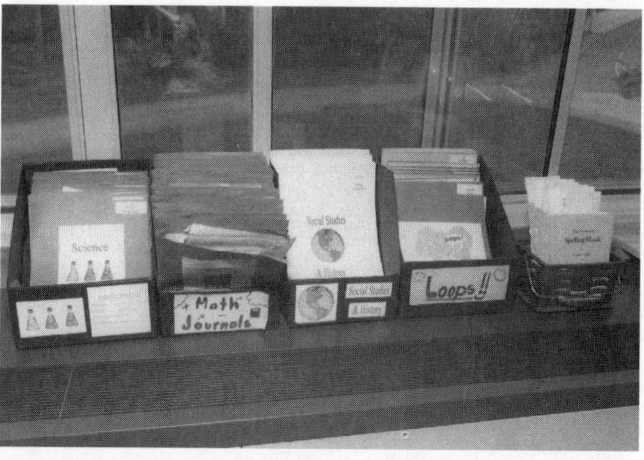

Storing student work by subject in different colored portfolios helps make this classroom organized and efficient.

For those who live in northern climes, the need to store heavy winter clothing and boots is a yearly headache. Coat hooks just don't hold a backpack, heavy coat, snow pants, and boots! Something is always on the floor, cluttering the pathway. One very effective solution I have seen is to give each student a thirty-gallon, drawstring trash bag with his or her name on it. Boots go in first, followed by the snow pants and jacket. The drawstring is pulled tight and the bag hung on the hook. Ta da! No clutter blocking the pathway to the door.

It may seem that I've made a lot of fuss over clutter and storage, and perhaps I have. But the fact of the matter is that reducing clutter and providing adequate storage are keys to creating positive vitality in your classroom. Lack of vitality in the classroom translates into difficulty moving around safely, a sense of unrest that can cause negative interactions, and a decreased ability to focus and work productively. Teachers have all experienced this dynamic, even if they can't put a name to it. Start tidying up today and notice the difference. When the things around you are in order, your life is in order and you can function more effectively. The same is true of your students. Teaching and learning will take off!

Your classroom is thoughtfully arranged with heartfelt intention. The energy in your room moves freely. Is there anything else to be considered? Hmm . . .

What about the Walls?

My guess is that most teachers do not have the luxury of selecting the color of their classroom walls unless the building is getting an overhaul. Even if this is the case, you still may not be given a choice. Feng shui consultant Laurie Biggers has selected what she feels is the "universal" classroom color. It begins with yellow or terra cotta, the earth tones, which exude a safe and supportive feeling. Then it is spiked with a touch of pink, from the element fire, which helps to keep everyone going but not too excited. What is the result of this blend of colors? It's a peachy shade.

If you are able to suggest a color for your classroom or have the freedom to paint it yourself, here are three suitable shades of peach to choose from. All three happen to be Sherwin Williams paints, but you can find similar shades in any brand of paint.

Light peach: Peachy SW1620

Darkish peach: Precious Peach SW1619

Brownish peach: Peach Sorbet SW1332

What you place on the walls and where you place it is as important as the wall color. As I mentioned earlier, put things you want your students to review and remember above eye level on the side walls. This stimulates the visual mode of recall (Jensen 1995).

Things that need to be communicated or talked about should be at eye level on the side walls of the classroom. The schedule for the day, important messages, assignments, and a How Do You Feel Today? chart are among the things you would place in this position (Jensen 1995). (See page 67 for instructions for making a How Do You Feel Today? chart.)

Posters containing positive messages, poetry, or affirmations are best placed high on the side or back walls. Affirmation posters are commercially available or you may create your own. (Better yet, make this a student project.) Print the affirmations in large letters on pastel poster board. Always phrase the affirmations positively, as if they were already true. Here are a few examples:

I am a capable learner.

I am a friend to everyone.

I am happy to be me!

My work is awesome!

Such posters help to instill a positive attitude and foster feelings of self-worth and confidence in your students, and of course, yourself. (How to use personal affirmations most effectively with your students is discussed beginning on page 115.)

Many of the things that you hang on or near the walls of your classroom will be expressions of the feng shui elements: wind chimes, wind socks, framed artwork, plants, and the like. These items help personalize your classroom space and create a nurturing and supportive environment for teaching and learning.

So you've analyzed your classroom from a feng shui perspective, and you're ready for your students . . . Well, almost. It's a good idea to take one last look at your classroom space. Here's where the Smile Test comes in.

The Smile Test

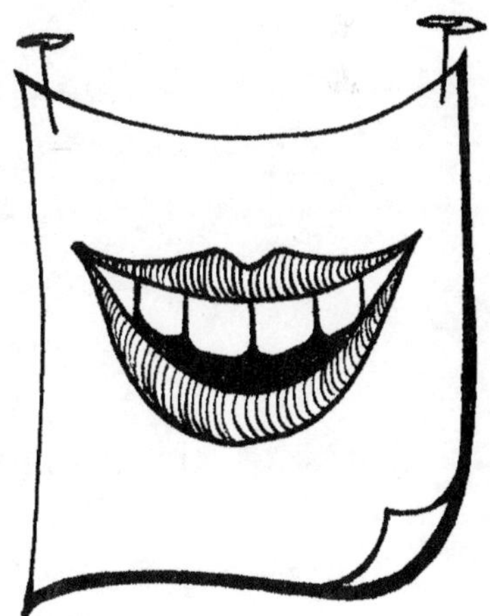

You've worked hard to create a nurturing and supportive classroom environment. Be sure it meets your needs and the needs of your students by giving it the **smile test.** Leave your classroom for a few minutes, closing the door behind you. When you return to your classroom, open the door with fresh eyes.

- How do you feel as you look into your room?
- Is your desk in a position of power where you can see the main doorway while sitting at it?
- Are the yin and yang spaces in your classroom well defined?
- Are the traffic patterns well defined for free energy flow?

- Does the student desk arrangement allow for seating flexibility and quick rearrangement if necessary?
- Are you smiling from the inside out as you look into your classroom?

Now, walk to the center of your room and carefully observe each area of it:

- Is anything distracting?
- Does any area need better organization?
- Does the student desk arrangement meet the needs of your students as you anticipate them?
- Have you provided a place for both yin and yang activities?
- Is the front of your room aesthetically pleasing and simply designed?
- Are things that need to be communicated or talked about placed at eye level on the side walls of the room?
- Are instructional charts located on the side walls above eye level?
- Are affirmations or positive posters placed above eye level on the side or back walls?
- Have you provided a time-out place and a private work space or spaces?
- As you look around your room, are you smiling from the inside out?

Make appropriate adjustments based on your responses to these questions. Then do the smile test again. If the smile is there, you are ready to go! Ta da! Now you are ready to move on to the pu pu platter, the dishes, or techniques, that help you take care of yourself.

Part II

Relaxing or Energizing Yourself for Optimum Teaching

You have created a supportive and nurturing classroom environment. You smile from the inside out when you walk in the door. You're ready to go! But it doesn't take long before you start to feel overburdened and stressed with paperwork, assessments, meetings, and unforeseen, *incredibly important,* must-have by 3:30 four-page surveys, not to mention the challenges of your personal life. None of this emotional clutter disappears in a puff of smoke just by wishing it away! So what can you do when stresses and challenges in your life cause emotional upsets that distract you from your teaching? Read on for some answers.

Chapter 3

The Breath

To my way of thinking, the most important technique you can learn to help yourself move through your emotions and distractions is the breath. It is a part of your every moment, day in and day out, wherever you are. The breath is your anchor to life, bringing you energy, vitality, clarity, and good health. By learning to work with it, you become able to change your state of being so you can function in a more balanced, efficient, and productive way.

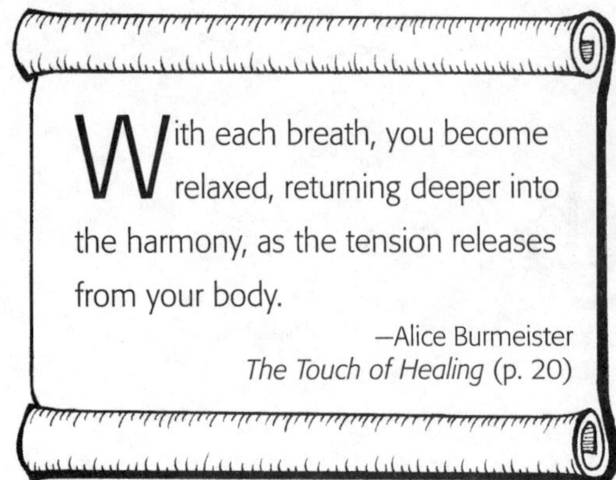

Not only will improved breathing help to change your state of being, it has physical benefits as well. Julie T. Lusk writes about the physical benefits of deep abdominal breathing in her book *Desktop Yoga* (1998), citing these changes:

- slowed heart rate
- increased lymphatic flow and transfer of oxygen from the blood into the body's tissues
- improved return of blood to the heart through the veins
- normalized flow of blood to the lungs
- increased blood and oxygen flow to the brain and the heart
- reduced tension and stress in the muscles
- pain reduction

The breath can empower you to transform yourself and your life.

How Do You Breathe?

Breathing is something we do automatically, day in and day out. Because it is automatic, we don't generally pay attention to it unless we are out of breath for some reason or have an illness that causes labored breathing. So take a few moments to notice how you breathe. You may do this experience sitting or lying down. If you choose to sit, make sure that your spine is straight and your feet are planted firmly on the floor. If you choose to lie down, you may wish to bend your legs at the knees to put less strain on your lower back and to place a rolled towel under your neck to support it, especially if you have neck problems.

1. Now, close your eyes and relax in this position. Breathe normally. Quiet your mind and pay attention to the sensations inside your body. Feel the breath going in and out, in and out, in and out. . . .
2. Notice your inhalation, how you draw breath in. With each breath, you receive oxygen and life-giving energy. Where do you feel the breath as it goes in? Are you relaxed as you breathe in? Or are you tense as you breathe in? If so, where do you feel tension? Do you breathe through your mouth or through your nose? What part(s) of your body expand with the inhalation?
3. Notice your exhalation, how you let out the breath. Each exhalation is a release, a letting go. Where do you feel the breath as it goes out? What part(s) of your body contract as you exhale?
4. Pay attention to your breathing. Notice your "in" breath. Notice your "out" breath. Learn about your breathing self. Are the inhalations and exhalations the same or different lengths? Are there times when you pause between the inhalation and exhalation? Are you relaxed as you breathe? Or are you tense as you breathe? Are you breathing from your upper chest or from down deep in your belly? Notice. Increase your awareness. Know your breathing self.

 *What did you notice about your breathing?*

Perhaps you noticed that you were breathing into your upper chest rather than deep into your belly. If so, you are an upper chest breather. Only a half-teacup of blood per minute flows through the upper part of your lungs, which is the least efficient place for oxygen to be transferred to the blood for circulation through the body. If you breathe deep into your belly, more than a liter of blood per minute flows into the bottom of your lungs, where the most efficient oxygen transfer takes place (Hendricks 1995).

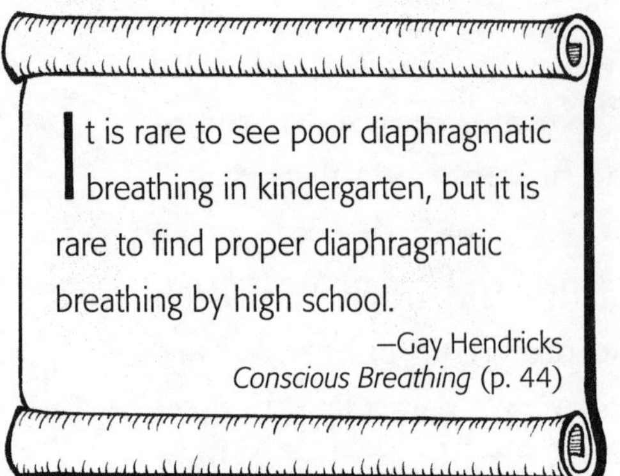

Your body will satisfy its oxygen and blood-flow needs. If you take shallow breaths into the upper lungs, you will take more shallow, tense breaths. If you take deep breaths into the lower lungs, you'll take fewer, more relaxed breaths. How would you prefer to breathe?

Good News

Like many of us, you may have just discovered that you are a half-teacup breather. Don't panic. All is not lost. You were once a liter breather and can become a liter breather again. It just takes remembering and practice.

Now some of us who have been around a good while have to go a bit farther back to remember than others. For a quick reminder of what liter breathing looks like, observe a newborn baby. A baby's belly rises and falls with each breath. It uses its lungs fully. So, you may ask, if we come into the world as liter breathers, why do we end up as half-teacup breathers?"

One answer is life. As we grow, we have life experiences that cause various feelings and sensations within our bodies. Feelings and sensations like tension and anxiety elicit a physical response that causes us to tighten our breathing. This tightening brings our breathing into the upper chest and the upper part of the lungs. When we have another stressful experience, cellular memory kicks in, and we go right back to that restricted breathing pattern. So the longer we have been alive, the stronger the cellular memory we have to repattern. But it can be done.

Our fast-paced lives, rushing from here to there, huffing and puffing along the way to get things done on time, also contributes to restricted breathing. Combine that hurried state with other possible dynamics, such as poor posture, tight clothing (Sarley and Sarley 1999), or a belief that we should hold our bellies in, a belief handed down from many mothers to their daughters and ever present in magazine ads showing flat-bellied male and female fashion models. Now we have multiplied the negative effects of cellular memory. Deep abdominal breathing is rare.

In order to change your breathing pattern, it is helpful to understand the role the diaphragm plays in your breathing health. Let's take a look.

The Role of the Diaphragm in Breathing

The diaphragm is a thin sheet of muscle fiber that separates the thoracic region (chest cavity), where your heart and lungs are housed, from the abdominal region (the belly), where other vital organs are housed. Shaped like a dome, it extends from front to back and from side to side. Gay Hendricks, author of *Conscious Breathing,* compares the diaphragm to the drumhead on a snare drum, albeit a very loose drumhead (Hendricks 1995).

Inhalation

As you breathe in, the dome of the diaphragm flattens, tightens, and is pulled downward. When the belly muscles are relaxed, the abdomen expands and the diaphragm tightens with each inhalation. This allows the lungs to expand fully and take in the maximum amount of oxygen. If the belly muscles are not relaxed, the diaphragm will not fully flatten, the belly will not fully rise, and the lungs will not receive as much oxygen (Hendricks 1995).

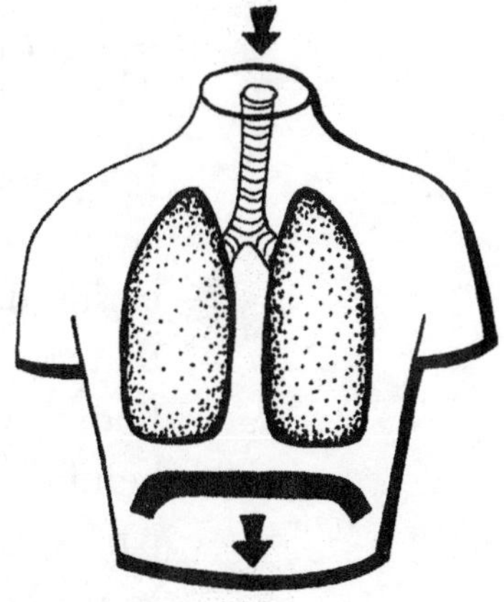

Exhalation

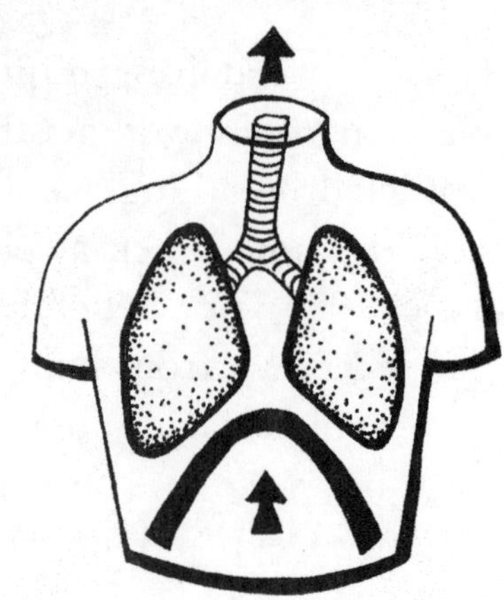

As you breathe out, the flattened diaphragm relaxes and returns to its resting arched position (Hendricks 1995). Exhaling completely releases the maximum amount of carbon dioxide from the lungs. Stale air is replaced with fresh air. By taking deep abdominal breaths, you allow your diaphragm to function optimally. The increased amount of oxygen taken into your lungs improves the oxygenation of all your body's organs, glands, and systems. Your heart doesn't have to work as hard to pump blood, and your brain has more oxygen to help you think and create. What's more, your vital organs receive a healthy massage!

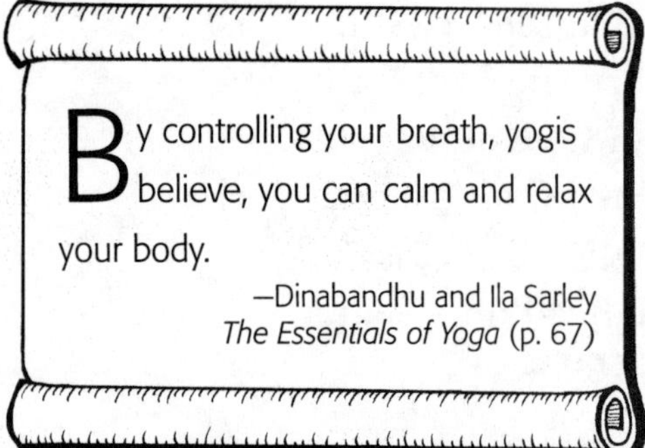

By controlling your breath, yogis believe, you can calm and relax your body.

—Dinabandhu and Ila Sarley
The Essentials of Yoga (p. 67)

By relearning deep abdominal breathing, you will enhance your circulation, your energy level, and your ability to concentrate (Sarley and Sarley 1999). You will be empowered to change your emotional state when you want to feel more calm and relaxed. Deep abdominal breathing will turn you into a healthy liter breather once again!

The How-to of Deep Abdominal Breathing

Deep abdominal breathing can best be learned in three stages. It is easiest to learn while lying on your back, but you may sit in a chair or stand up if you prefer. If you choose to sit or stand, make sure that your spine is straight and your feet are planted firmly on the floor. If you prefer to lie down, you may be most comfortable if you bend your knees and place your feet flat on the floor, to ease lower back strain (as illustrated previously). Placing a rolled towel under your neck can ease neck strain.

Stage I: Abdominal Region Inflation

1. Once you are in a comfortable position, place your hands on your belly. You may wish to close your eyes.
2. Imagine that there is a balloon inside your body, filling your chest and belly. As you breathe in through your nose, visualize filling the lower part of the balloon, the lower lobes of your lungs, with the breath. Feel your belly expand as you breathe in. If your belly muscles are too tight to let your belly expand, gently push the belly out until your muscles relax and soften (Rutt n.d.). If you are still having trouble, place one hand about an inch away from your belly and inhale to make your belly touch your hand.
3. Exhale through your nose and visualize the balloon deflating as your belly flattens.

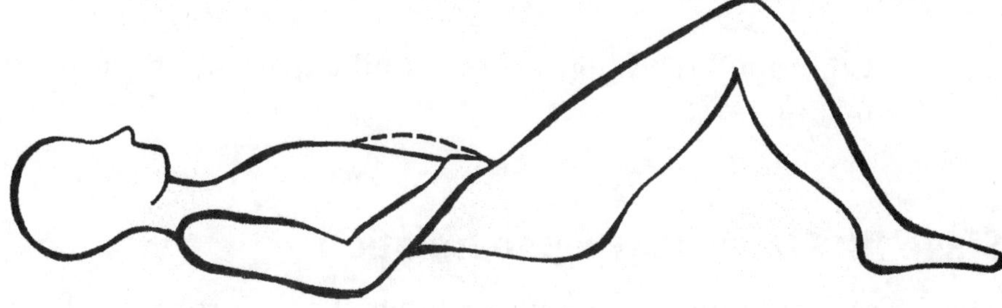

4. Repeat several times, noticing the expansion of your belly as you breathe in and the flattening of your belly as you breathe out.

Stage II: Thoracic Region Inflation

Now, let's attend to the expansion of the chest cavity as you inhale.

1. Continue in the same position as for stage I. Place your hands against your sides, a couple of inches above your waist.
2. Inhale through your nose, filling up the abdominal cavity and the lower lungs (the lower part of the balloon). Then imagine the breath moving up and filling the middle area of the balloon, the chest cavity.

3. Notice how your hands move outward as the diaphragm flattens and the rib cage expands to fill the middle part of your lungs, the chest cavity.
4. Now, notice your hands moving inward as you exhale through your nose and your diaphragm rounds again (Rutt n.d.). Remember, exhalation is a releasing process. Just let your breath flow gently out, rather than forcing it.

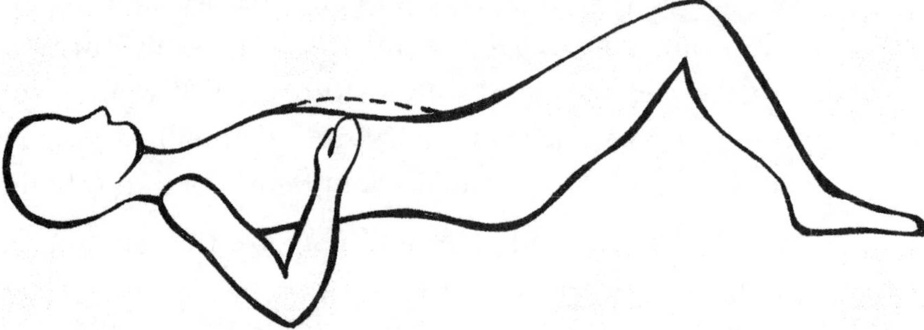

5. Continue breathing this way until expanding your chest feels natural and easy.

Stage III: Clavicular Region Inflation

Now let's pay attention to the upper lungs. This is probably where most of your inhalation has been occurring if you are a half-teacup breather:

1. Continuing in the same position, place your fingertips on the clavicle (collarbone) with the palm of your hand resting on your upper chest (Marina Walker, personal communication).
2. Inhale through your nose, filling the abdominal and thoracic regions as before and allowing the breath to fill up the top part of your lungs, the clavicular region, completely filling the balloon (Rutt n.d.). You will notice that your collarbone rises only slightly as the upper chest expands. If you have difficulty feeling this slight movement, place your fingertips on the top part of your sternum (the breastbone). Be sure that your shoulders remain relaxed as you inhale.

3. Exhale through your nose and let the lungs release the breath from the upper chest down through the clavicular, thoracic, and abdominal regions, deflating the balloon from the top down. Pull your navel in toward your spine at the end of the exhalation for full deflation of the lungs. Your diaphragm returns to its rounded position.

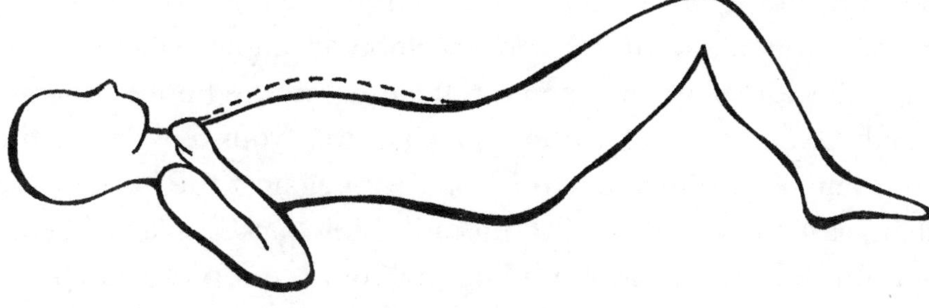

4. Repeat, combining the abdominal, chest, and upper chest parts together in a smooth, full inhalation and exhalation of the breath. Make each inhalation and exhalation the same duration.
5. Start by breathing in for a count of four, then exhaling for the same count. Work up to eight counts in and eight counts out. Again, keep your shoulders relaxed and let your clavicle rise slightly for full inhalation. Pull your navel in toward your spine at the end of the exhalation.
6. Exhaling air forcefully through your mouth can release anxiety, frustration, or anger. Keep the inhalation long and smooth as before.

Refer to the book *Breathwalk*, by Gurucharan Singh Khalsa, Ph.D., and Yogi Bhajan, Ph.D., to find out how using primal sounds or phonemes (the simplest speech units) can increase the effectiveness of the 4/4 and 8/8 breathing patterns.

8–4–8 Breathing

This breathing technique is very easy to master and offers a number of benefits (Rutt, personal communication). It helps keep the nervous system healthy, has a calming effect on the emotions, and encourages balanced functioning of the body's systems.

Begin by sitting on the floor in a comfortable pose with your legs crossed. You may want to sit on a cushion or pillow to elevate your hips. Sit with your spine straight. If sitting on the floor is uncomfortable, you may prefer to sit in a chair with your feet flat on the floor and your spine straight. Don't lean against the back of the chair, as generally this will result in leaning back instead of being upright. Imagine a string pulling up from the top of your head, straightening your spine. Use deep abdominal breathing as you learned to do in the last exercise.

1. Close your mouth and inhale for a silent count of eight. Feel the sternum, or breastbone, lift as you inhale.
2. Suspend the breath for a silent count of four. This is best accomplished by raising the chest slightly so that the throat and neck are not tight (Khalsa and Bhajan 2000). Keep your shoulders relaxed rather than letting them rise up toward your neck.
3. Place the tip of your tongue on the ridge of soft tissue that separates your teeth from the roof of your mouth and exhale through your nose for a silent count of eight. Feel the sternum fall, returning to the resting state, as you exhale. This completes one breathing cycle.
4. Repeat the 8–4–8 breathing pattern in smooth, flowing cycles.

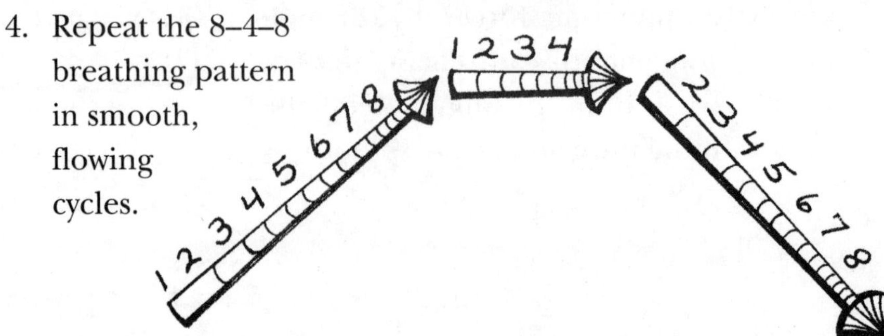

Are you wondering what the purpose of suspending the breath is? According to Gurucharan Singh Khalsa and Yogi Bhajan, suspending the breath "increases the utilization of oxygen in your system" (Khalsa and Bhajan 2000, 269). As you master this breathing pattern, you may gradually make each component the same length, eight counts in, eight counts suspended, and eight counts out. In addition to increasing the oxygenation benefits to your body, this longer suspension will be more relaxing as well.

Breath of Fire

Another yoga breathing technique is called **breath of fire.** Unlike deep abdominal breathing, it is strong and forceful. Once again, begin by sitting with a straight spine. Because this breathing pattern is a little bit more difficult to do and learn, I will pass along the instructions yoga teacher Stephanie Rutt gives her students to help ease them into this pattern.

1. Begin by doing deep abdominal breathing with inhalations and exhalations of equal duration. Gradually shorten the length of each inhalation and exhalation, allowing your breaths to become shallower and more rapid. Keep the inhalations and exhalations of equal length. Let your breath find its own rhythm. It should be effortless yet powerful.
2. With practice, the rhythm of your breath will quicken, becoming no deeper than sniffing. Throughout, the chest remains still and should be slightly raised. All the movement when inhaling and exhaling is in the abdomen, as the navel point is pulled in toward the spine. (Hint: Think of exhaling with enough energy to blow out a candle.) If you begin to feel dizzy, slow the pace and become aware of your inhalations and exhalations. Make sure that they are of equal duration. If necessary, stop the breathing pattern.
3. Continue this breathing pattern for one minute at first, gradually working up to three minutes.

To ensure that you are doing this breathing technique correctly, Khalsa and Bhajan (2000) recommend that you place one hand on your chest and the other between your navel point and your solar plexus. The solar plexus lies a couple of inches below your sternum, the tip of your breastbone. As you do the breath of fire, the hand on your chest should remain still and the hand on your upper abdomen should move in and out. Should you find it difficult to learn this breathing technique, consider taking a kundalini yoga class to learn it.

Why use breath of fire? The benefits are many. In *Breathwalk,* Khalsa and Bhajan (2000, 82) list these:

- stress release
- expanded lung capacity and vital breath
- expulsion of toxins from the lung tissues
- clearing of the mucous membranes
- alertness, energy, and strength
- "signature of wellness" in your body rhythms, such as your heartbeat
- balance in the autonomic nervous system
- loss of addictive impulses

The breath is fundamental for personal health and well-being. It is the anchor that brings you back to stillness in meditation, the self-help technique I will present in chapter 4.

Chapter 4

Meditation

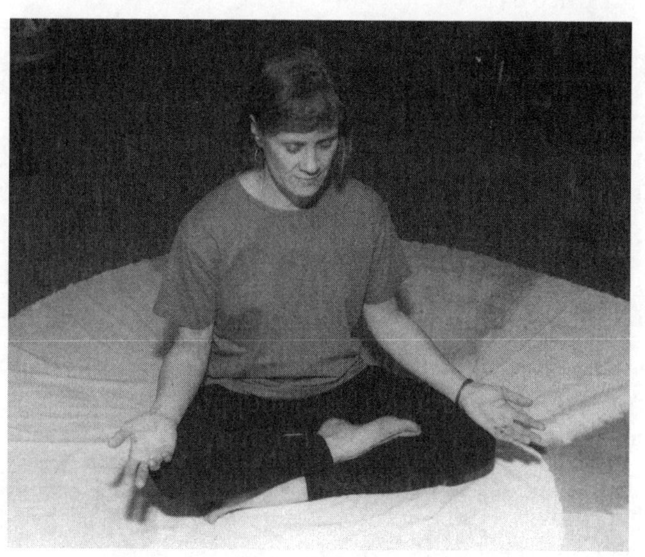

Why is meditation beneficial? The benefit lies in making a conscious decision to stop whatever you are doing and reach a state of stillness. For a moment, you get off the treadmill of life. You let go of the stack of papers that need grading. You let go of the planning you need to do for the science unit you start next week. You let go of the parent conference that is scheduled after school tomorrow. Instead, you spend some time in stillness, being in the moment, paying attention without judgment. The act of being still brings calm and relaxation to all aspects of your being: body, mind, and spirit. You can go back to your work rejuvenated.

In meditation, you are still, silently observing your thoughts, feelings, and sensations. Imagine that you are inside the security of your home, looking out the window at a driving rainstorm. You are behind the window, separated from the driving rain. Similarly, in meditation you are in a secure place behind your thoughts, feelings, and sensations, witnessing them rather than being in them, the driving rainstorm.

Being still is not easy, for your thoughts, feelings, and sensations are constantly pelting you like rain beating against the window, distracting you from your state of stillness. But you are wrapped in the stability and security of your home, secure on its foundation, which brings you back to being a witness rather than being caught up in the storminess of your life. Each time you get entangled with the happenings of the day or a disagreement with a colleague, you can go back to your foundation, the breath, the inhalation and exhalation, and return to stillness.

In sum, the goal of meditation is to consciously decide to stop doing anything, bringing yourself to stillness for no reason other than to be with each life-giving breath in the present moment. When you do this, you will receive the benefits of deep relaxation and inner peace. In time, you may even experience deep insights. By establishing a meditation practice, you are valuing and nurturing yourself. You are taking care of someone very important—you!

Establishing a Meditation Practice

With regard to meditation, the word *practice* does not mean working toward perfection. Instead, it means habitual action. Establishing a meditation practice means that you habitually and intentionally stop what you are doing to be present in the moment, to be aware. The result of practice is that you bring increased awareness and calmness into your everyday life as well. This transfer will strengthen your teaching.

The How-to of Sitting Meditation

1. Consciously decide to sit in a place that feels right to you. Some people create a sacred space at home with a lighted candle and other special objects, but it is unlikely you can do this at your workplace. Sitting outdoors or near a window where you can see the natural world are other good options.
2. As you seat yourself, whether it be on the floor or in a chair, do so with reverence. You are making a physical statement about your intention simply to be in the moment.
3. Sit on your cushion or chair in a "dignified posture," as Jon Kabat-Zinn, author of *Wherever You Go There You Are,* describes it. You will find that your head, neck, and spine will automatically find a place of alignment.

Establishing a meditation practice means that you habitually and intentionally stop what you are doing to be present in the moment, to be aware.

4. You may hold your hands in any of a variety of positions, called **mudras.** Try them and see what feels comfortable. It may be that you will decide to use different mudras at different times, if you find that each creates a particular kind of experience or feeling for you.
   - Place your hands palms down on your knees, a symbol of acceptance.

- Place your hands palms up on your knees, a symbol of receptivity.
- Place your hands in your lap with the fingers of the left hand overlapping the fingers of the right. The tips of your thumbs should be close together but not touching. If you lose your focus during meditation, the thumb tips will touch, reminding you to come back to focus, stillness (Stephanie Rutt, personal communication).
- Place your open hands palm up on your knees with the thumb and index finger of each hand touching, creating a circle. In yoga, this position is called **gyan mudra,** known as the mudra of wisdom, and symbolizes the principle that what goes around comes around (Stephanie Rutt, personal communication).

5. Close your eyes and imagine a tiny elevator inside your body, running from your tailbone to the top of your head, your mind. Take three deep abdominal breaths, and on your third deep breath, ride the elevator up from your tailbone to your mind. As you exhale, let your awareness take the elevator down from your mind to your heart center. Literally feel the elevator drop down into your heart.
6. Keep your awareness in your heart center and tune in to your natural breathing rhythm, the in and out of your breath. Breathe in and out through your nose. Be with the breath, and if your mind entangles you in the day's activities, just refocus on the breath again without judging or scolding yourself.
7. Begin small. If meditation is new to you, you might start with three to five minutes and gradually work up to twenty or thirty minutes.

8. As you begin to feel that you are ready to end your meditation time, stay seated a bit longer, then consciously decide to end the session. This transition helps to bring conscious closure to your sitting in a way that an abrupt, "OK, I'm done" finish does not (Kabat-Zinn 1994). Meditation, like a story, has a beginning, a middle, and an ending. Make them well defined. Leave your cushion or chair with reverence, just as you did when you sat down.

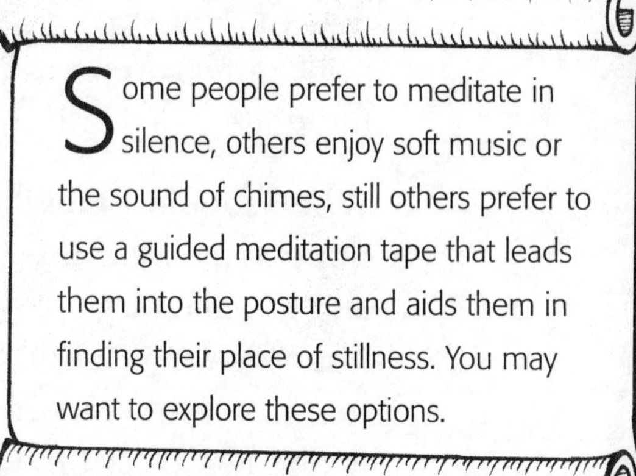

The Ins and Outs of Meditation

How long should I sit in meditation? The intention you bring to your meditation is more important than the length of time you sit. Five minutes of practice may have a greater effect than thirty minutes, especially if a long period of sitting is interrupted by children's questions or constant thoughts of what you have to do. Flexibility is important. If five minutes is what you have, that's great. And if you can carve out only a minute, celebrate the time you have. You have valued yourself by taking time to **stop and be,** however long you have. The rewards are great—inner peace, calm, clarity, and self-awareness—and will become deeper as you are able to increase your meditation time.

The intention you bring to your meditation is more important than the amount of time you sit.

Should I meditate in silence or with sound? Again, there is no right or wrong choice. If you are new to meditation, soft instrumental music may help you to relax. I started meditating that way myself, but now I prefer silence. Some prefer the sound of a bell or chimes, while others prefer to be led in meditation. (See the Resource List for guided meditations.)

When should I meditate? Some people advocate meditating first thing in the morning, because it helps you start your day in a calm and balanced state. I concur, but sometimes meditating first thing just doesn't work out for one reason or another. So work meditation into your day whenever it will fit. Just as there is no right or wrong length of time to meditate, so is there no right or wrong time of day. In fact, going back to the breath throughout the day is rejuvenating. Be kind to yourself. Let go of any attachment to the length of time, when, and where you meditate. Give yourself the gift of self-awareness. Just do it!

By consciously taking the time to stop and be still, this teacher rejuvenates herself so she can continue teaching in a calmer, more relaxed way.

Another practice that makes use of the breath and relaxes the body is yoga. It just might be your cup of tea.

Chapter 5

Yoga

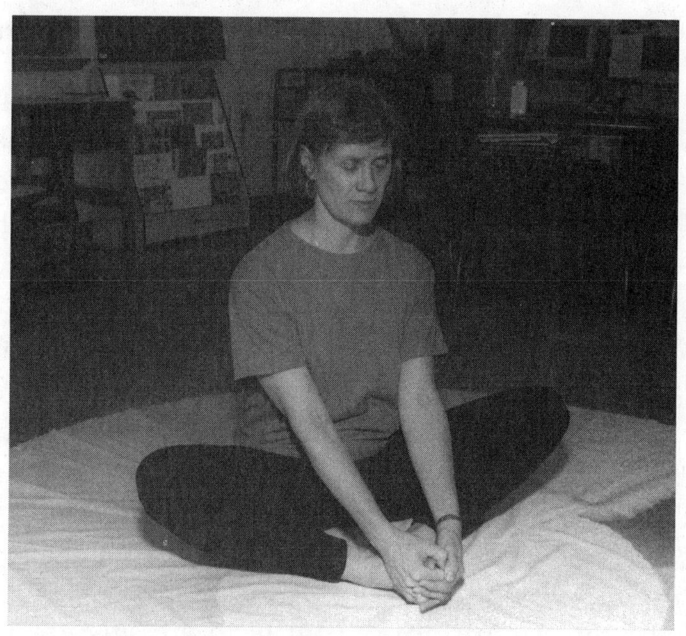

When the stresses at school are threatening to take over your life, try yoga. It is one of the best stress reducers around, because it promotes relaxation by calming the nervous system. Other benefits include enhancing your flexibility and increasing your strength, vitality, and energy (Sarley and Sarley 1999). Certainly, the practice of yoga can be a healing force in your life that helps you relax or feel revitalized and move into a more positive way of being.

Like meditation, yoga is a way of taking time out to nurture yourself, to be in the moment. In *The Essentials of Yoga,* Dinabandhu Sarley and Ila Sarley write that holding a posture helps you to "learn about the sensation of focus. You experience yourself as a person who is focused. . . . When you are developing a sense of balance in order to hold a yoga posture, you are learning what it feels like, inside, to be balanced" (Sarley and Sarley 1999, 30). You can learn to call upon this sensation any time you need to get back on track, respond to life in a calmer way, or get back to what needs doing.

Many health clubs and studios offer yoga classes, and you may enjoy signing up for a class. In this chapter, I will focus on some practices you can use at school without a mat or change of clothes. All you need is a chair and a few minutes during your planning time, at lunch, or even with your students during class time. Give yourself the gift of mindful movement by trying the following stretches and postures. Notice how you feel before and after doing these stretches and postures.

These stretches may be done while either standing or sitting, whichever you prefer. If you stand, you will need to plant your feet firmly, no more than shoulder width apart, so your weight is distributed evenly on the balls and heels of your feet. Stand with your spine straight and the crown (top) of your head pressing upward, eyes straight ahead, and arms at your sides with the palms facing in. Keeping your knees soft, slightly bent rather than locked straight, will help to bring your body into alignment. If you prefer to sit, sit upright on a chair, feet planted firmly on the floor, spine straight and crown pressing upward, head and eyes forward, and arms at your sides with the palms facing in.

Before beginning any yoga stretches or postures, center yourself by bringing your attention inward. Use deep abdominal breathing or the elevator visualization to help you come to your center. Doing this will relax your muscles and slow your heart rate. Remember always to inhale and exhale through your nose, and to stretch only as far as is comfortable.

Forehead Stretch

The forehead stretch relieves the tension you may feel around your eyes and in the muscles of your forehead.

1. Place your thumbs on your temples and let the tips of your fingers meet in the center of your forehead.
2. Draw your fingertips across your forehead toward your temples. As you draw your fingers across your forehead, visualize the tightness being drawn out and released. Repeat several times.
3. Coordinating your breathing with the movement helps you visualize and increases relaxation. Inhale while holding your fingertips together in the center of your forehead, and as you exhale, draw your fingers across your forehead, visualizing the tightness being drawn out and released. Then inhale as you bring your fingertips back to the center of your forehead and exhale as you draw them out again.
4. While your fingertips are at your temples, gently massage them in little circles to relax your eyes.

Chest and Back Stretches

Many people feel discomfort in the chest and back. The following stretches will help to open up your chest, relax the muscles in your back, and stretch your spine.

Chest Opener

1. Sit or stand with a straight spine and your feet parallel, shoulder width apart. Focus your eyes forward and let your arms hang relaxed at your sides, palms in. If you are standing, keep your knees soft and slightly bent. This stretch is probably easiest to do standing up. A stool works best if you prefer to be sitting. If you sit on a chair, you will need to sit sideways so that the back of the chair does not interfere with the movement of your arms.

2. Inhale deeply, then as you exhale, clasp your hands behind your back, resting them on your buttocks. Squeeze your shoulder blades together.
3. On your next inhalation, raise your hands and arms off your buttocks, keeping your shoulder blades together. Feel the front of your chest expand with the breath.
4. Stay in this posture, breathing deeply several times.
5. When you are ready to finish, inhale and on the exhalation, release your hands and let your arms fall loosely to your sides, palms in. Stay in this relaxed position while you return to breathing normally.

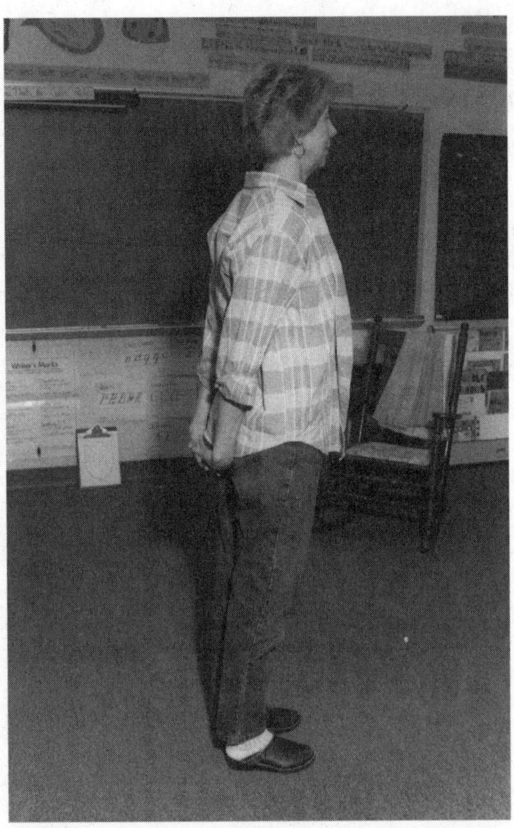

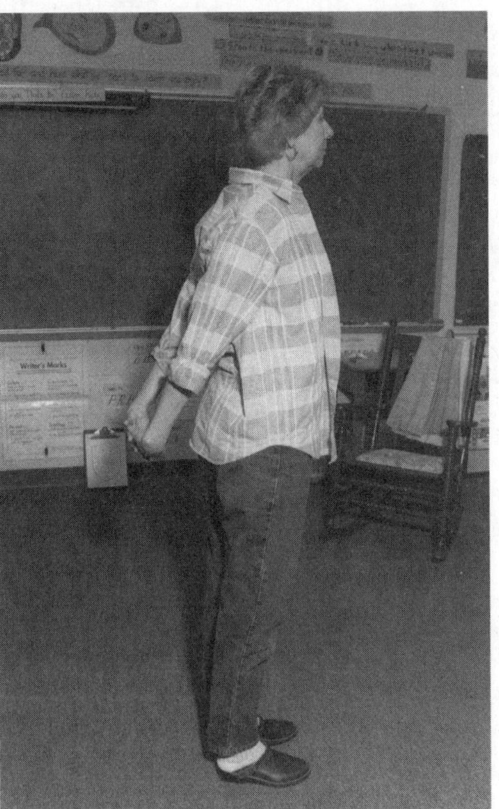

The chest opener stretch releases tension in your chest.

Modified Child Pose

The modified child pose helps to stretch out the muscles along your spine and lengthen it.

1. Sit on a chair with your spine straight and the crown of your head pressed upward, feet separated slightly and planted firmly on the floor. Look straight ahead and let your arms hang at your sides, palms in.
2. Inhale deeply and on the exhalation, slowly lower your chest to your thighs. Let your head and neck hang forward over your knees and your hands drop to the floor, like a rag doll.
3. Stay in this position, breathing deeply. You may notice that with each exhalation, your chest sinks a little farther toward your thighs.
4. When your stretch feels complete, inhale then slowly come back to a seated position as you exhale, unfurling your spine one vertebra at a time, starting at the tailbone. Stay in this relaxed position for a few moments before moving on.

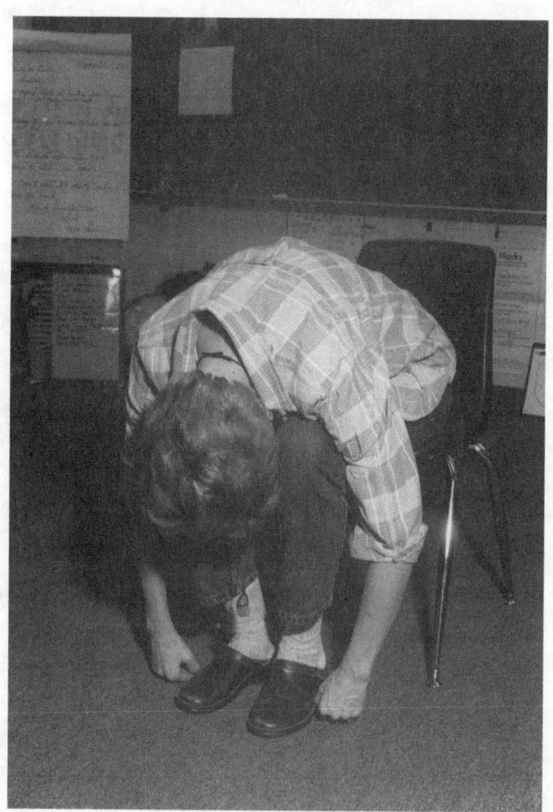

The modified child pose stretches the muscles along your spine, reducing tension.

Seated Spinal Twist

The seated spinal twist helps to keep your spine flexible and reduces tightness.

1. Sit on a chair with a back. Face forward and lengthen your spine toward the ceiling. Plant your feet directly under your knees, that is, shoulder width apart. Place your right hand on your left thigh.
2. Inhale deeply, and as you exhale, slowly twist to the left from the base of your spine, placing your left hand on the back of the chair. Continue twisting until your eyes are gazing over your left shoulder or you have turned as far as you can go comfortably. Keep your chest open, your shoulders relaxed, and your chin level.
3. Stay in this position, breathing deeply. When you are ready to release the position, inhale, and as you exhale turn back to face forward.
4. Repeat this sequence on the right side, placing your left hand on your right thigh and your right hand on the back of the chair.

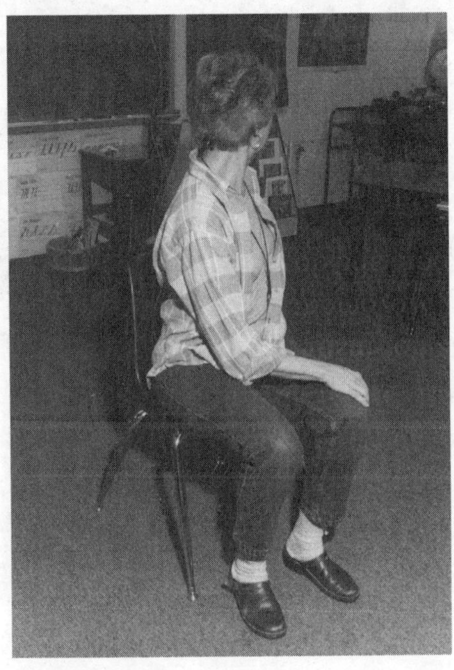

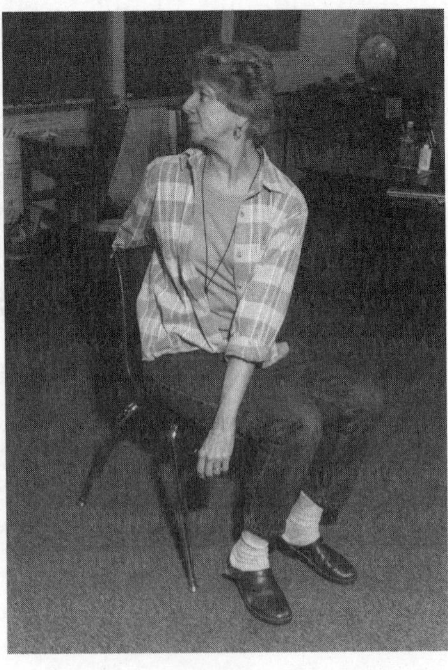

The seated spinal twist is a great way to release tension in your back.

Standing Forward Bend

For this lower back stretch, plant your feet shoulder width apart with your knees soft, slightly bent. Stand looking straight ahead, with your spine straight and your shoulders relaxed. Let your arms hang relaxed at your sides with the palms facing in.

1. Inhale, then as you exhale slowly, bend at the hips and allow your arms to dangle, heavy and long. Let the weight of your head draw your spine downward as far as you can go comfortably. It is important to keep your knees soft and slightly bent, your torso as close to your thighs as possible, and your neck and arms relaxed.
2. While in this position, take long, deep abdominal breaths. Sighing loudly on each exhalation helps to release the tension trapped inside your body.
3. After you have taken several deep breaths, inhale deeply one last time, and on the exhalation, straighten slowly, one vertebra at a time, starting at the tailbone. Stand in a relaxed position for a few moments before resuming your day.

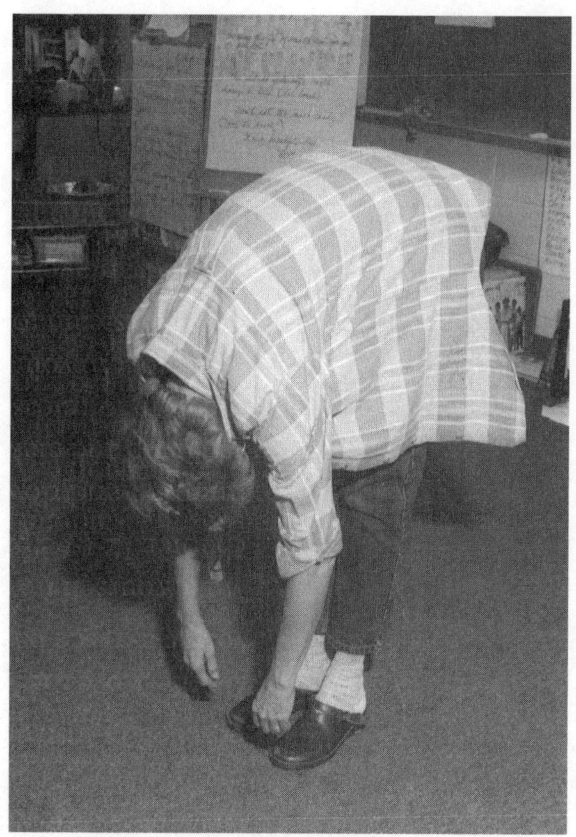

The standing forward bend helps to loosen the muscles in your lower back. Standing with your feet shoulder width apart, rather than together, will give you more stability.

Another way to relax and improve your focus is Reiki. In chapter 6, I will introduce you to this traditional healing technique.

Chapter 6

Reiki

Reiki, an ancient hands-on healing practice, can reduce your stress and boost your energy level. It was first recorded in the Tibetan **Sutras,** *ancient records of philosophy and cosmology, and was rediscovered at the end of the nineteenth century by Dr. Mikao Usui of Kyoto, Japan.*

Reiki *is a compound of two words that express its meaning:* rei *and* ki. **Rei** *means "universal" and refers to all of creation: humans, plants, animals, the stars, and the planets.* **Ki** *means "life energy," the energy that gives life to all of creation. This energy is within and all around us.* Chi *and* prana *are other commonly used words for this energy from the Chinese and Hindu cultures, respectively.*

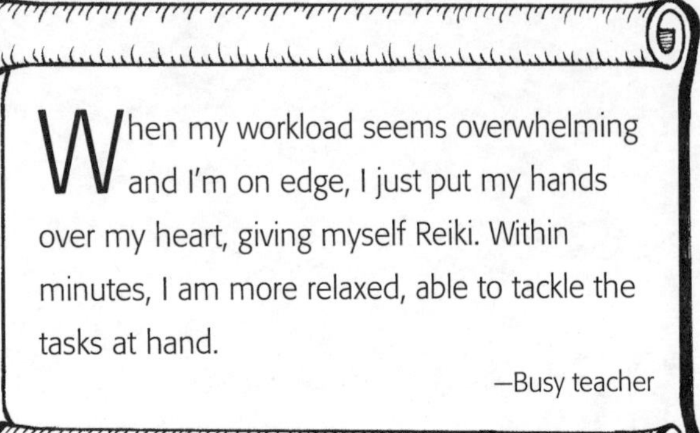

What does this universal energy feel like? If you take your hands and hold them as if there were a softball between them, you might be able to sense the energy. Do this now. Try moving your hands in and out, making the ball larger and smaller. Moving your hands in and out is like pulling taffy; you can feel a stretching. Sometimes, the energy is felt as a thickness or warmth between the hands.

You can harness the universal energy to bring balance into your body. The practitioner giving you Reiki, who may be yourself or someone else, comes with the intention to be of service to you in your healing and to act as a channel for the universal energy. When your body receives the energy, your higher intelligence transforms it into healing energy and uses it for your highest good at that moment to bring you into balance on all levels: physical, mental, emotional, and spiritual. So, it might be that the stomachache you arrived at the session with might not be relieved. Instead, you may find an answer to a problem you have been pondering.

One of the most significant overall benefits of receiving Reiki is that it relaxes the body. If you are feeling uptight or uneasy about something, all you have to do is put your hands where you are feeling the sensation, and within a short time you will usually feel your discomfort fade away. Reiki empowers you to take care of yourself and your state of being no matter where you are: to calm yourself in the classroom, to relax at home after a busy day, or to give yourself an energy boost whenever you are feeling tired. All you need are your hands, and they are always with you wherever and whenever you need them! With Reiki, you are empowered to take charge of your life and your emotions. This technique is all about unconditional love, nurturing yourself, and bringing yourself to wholeness.

If you are interested in learning to do Reiki, you will need to find a Reiki Master to train you. Check at your local health food stores or New Age stores or on the Internet for Reiki organizations that can refer you to a Reiki Master in your area.

Reiki and ADHD

I would like to comment here on the use of Reiki with ADHD children. For some ADHD children I have worked with, Reiki has been a useful tool in helping them control their emotions and behaviors. One student, who was not on medication, was able to self-regulate in school. He would place his hands on his body wherever he felt the sensation that indicated he was in need of control. For him, this site was typically either in his stomach or his head. If he felt the sensation in his stomach, he would cross his arms over his belly and lean against his desk. When he felt the sensation in his head, he would place his elbow on his desk and rest his head in his hand, covering the area of discomfort. He was able to assume these postures subtly, without drawing attention to himself, because both are common ways of sitting. Yet, he was feeding his body's cells with healing energy, diminishing the sensations he was feeling and bringing inner calm. By tuning in to his body, understanding its signals, he was able to maintain better control on his own without outside intervention or medication.

This particular boy had the support of his mother, who gave him daily Reiki treatments before he went to school, concentrating on his head, stomach, and feet. Treating his feet helped ground him, connecting him to the earth. Parental support is essential if Reiki is to become a positive force in a child's life, and this mother's commitment was instrumental in her son's success. Parents can help their children learn to recognize the internal sensations that indicate a disruption is imminent, and can cue them to do Reiki before it happens. Just saying the child's name and either putting your

A fourth-grade student gives herself Reiki when she is angry. She says her head feels like it's going to explode, so she puts her hands on her cheeks for a moment, then pulls them down off her face. It's like she is pulling the anger out of her head.

hands over your heart or saying, "Do Reiki," is all that is necessary. Teachers can cue their Reiki-trained students in the same way. Ideally, as children mature, they will be increasingly able to self-regulate as they become aware of the sensations that signal impending loss of control. Reiki is one part of the solution for these children and is a gift that lasts a lifetime.

Interactions between children with ADHD and their parents or teachers can quickly escalate out of control. Reiki can help the adults around a child with ADHD calm themselves so this doesn't happen. By staying calm the adults are better able to respond positively to the child—which is, of course, in everyone's best interest.

In my experience, Reiki has proven beneficial for children with ADHD, their parents, and their siblings. Parents reported that they were more tolerant and accepting of the child with ADHD and their other children as well. The children with ADHD felt calmer, had a greater sense of self-worth, and didn't get into trouble at school as frequently. Both adults and children had better control over their behaviors.

As a teacher, you have the opportunity to influence your students' lives in many ways and to suggest various solutions to your students' problems. Reiki is an option you can offer a parent of a child with ADHD. Certainly, it is the parent's choice whether or not to pursue your suggestion, but you will have planted a seed that may, over time, germinate and grow. And aren't we all about supporting our students' growth in every way?

The techniques I have covered thus far are the quiet, yin type. Movement is an active, yang technique, which at times may be just what you need to do your best work!

Chapter 7

Get Up and Move

Eric Jensen, author of Super Teaching, *recommends taking an oxygen break every fifteen minutes or so. But how am I supposed to do that when I barely have time to slip off to the bathroom? you ask. When you consider that oxygen breaks will help to keep you alert and energized, I'm sure you will be open to finding ways to fit them into your school day. Incidentally, another tip is to make sure you drink plenty of water, as dehydration can leave you feeling lethargic and headachy.*

Here are a few options for taking a brief movement break:

- Take an oxygen break when you feel the need. Chances are that a good many of your students will need one too! Do a bit of stretching, marching in place, or moving around the room to the beat of a percussion instrument.
- Tune into your students' energy levels and take an oxygen break when they look or act depleted. You could probably use a break then too! Again, do a bit of stretching, marching in place, or moving around the room to the beat of a percussion instrument.
- Do the Move the Way You Feel exercise, either alone or with your class (see page 125).
- Wake yourself up by doing the Isolations series described in chapter 12 (see page 127).
- Jump up and down ten times. Reach up with your arms as you jump and make a sound if you are so inclined! The sound will help to release tension from your body. Invite your students to join you. It gives them a chance to be noisy and let off some steam too!
- Take advantage of your trips to the office, another teacher's room, or the bathroom to walk briskly (consistent with observing your school's rules about moving safely in the building).
- Take a brisk five-minute walk around the classroom when your students are out of the room with a specialist. If you can walk outside, all the better!
- Play some uplifting music such as *Mozart in Motion* (volume 3 of the Mozart Effect series compiled by Don Campbell). Move to the music to get your circulation going.

For those of you who are able to find a block of time before or after school, look into the Breathwalk program developed by Gurucharan Singh Khalsa, Ph.D., and Master of Kundalini Yoga Yogi Bhajan, Ph.D. Breathwalk combines controlled breathing with walking and focusing. You coordinate your steps with specific breathing patterns to exercise your physical body, use your meditative abilities, and relax your mind.

> Movement is not only essential for nerve net development and thought, but also for adequate heart and lung development to support brain function.
>
> —Carla Hannaford, *Smart Moves* (p. 146)

For those of you who prefer simply to walk, consider having a group of older students with math talents create an indoor walking course in your building. Have them mark off a course and create a map for distribution to the teachers. A walking path right in the hallway will make exercising easier! It does not matter *how* you choose to move, what matters is that you do it. Movement revitalizes you so you can be fully present in your classroom and do your best teaching.

Now for Part III, a pu pu platter of techniques that you can use with your students.

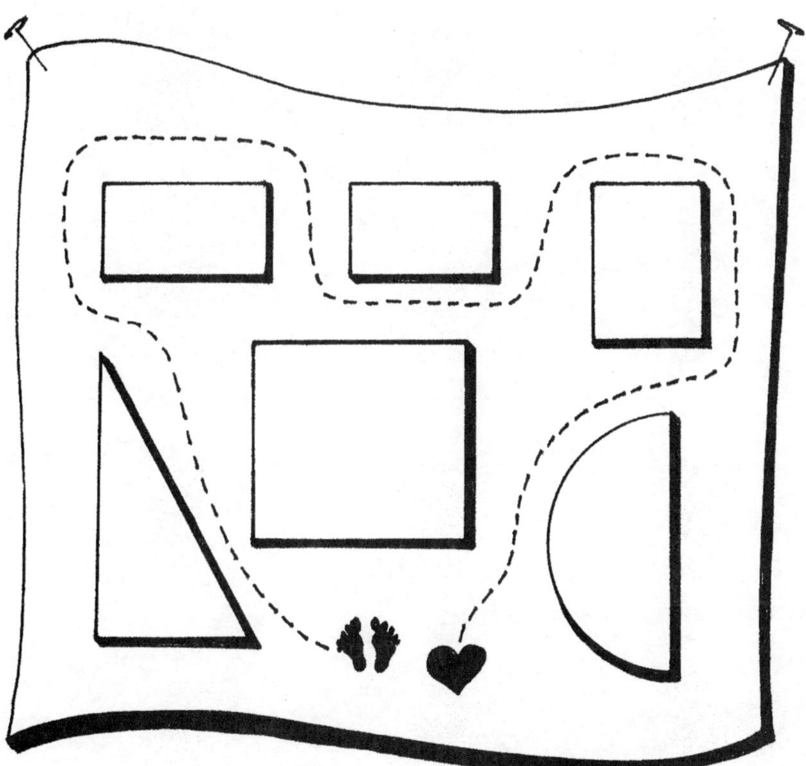

Part III

Relaxing or Energizing Your Students for Optimum Learning

The room is ready, nurturing, and supportive. You are ready, relaxed, and energized, and your students are about to enter. Your classroom space is about to become a classroom community. What can you do to help your students stay focused and alert so they can do their best work? Read on for some answers.

Chapter 8

Taking the Emotional Temperature of Your Class

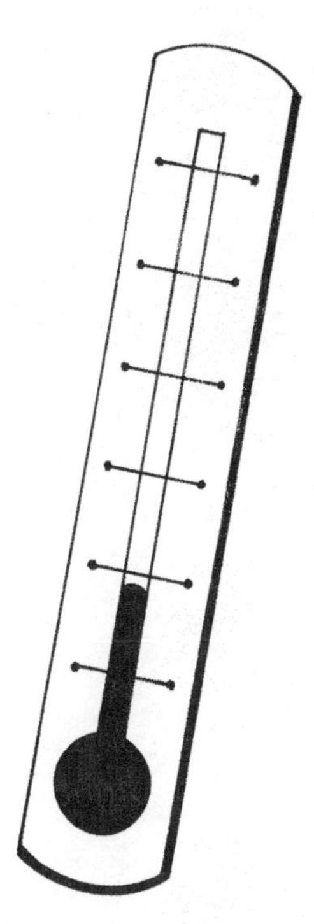

Just as you walk into your classroom in various states of being, so do your students. Many are tired from a long bus ride, others have had an early-morning battle with a sibling, and still others might come to school saddened by any number of events in their personal lives. You hope most will enter the classroom in good spirits. Whatever the case may be, tuning in to the emotional temperature of your students, both individually and collectively, as they enter the classroom allows you to take measures to enhance their state of being so they can do their best work. Here are a few ways you might register the emotional temperatures of your students:

1. If possible, greet your students at the door. You can often tell from their tone of voice when they say hello or their body language as they enter where they are on the emotional thermometer. Make a mental note of this so you can help individual students or the class as a whole as soon as possible. Greeting students at the door is also a great way to enhance the sense of connectedness and community in your class.
2. For an elementary classroom, you might create a How Do You Feel Today? chart that students, you, and any other adults who spend a good deal of time in your classroom can use to indicate how they feel. (Faces with different expressions are used to indicate everyone's emotional state.) Instructions for making and using such a chart are given in the lesson plan that follows.
3. An alternative to using faces for the How Do You Feel Today? chart is to have students use the stoplight colors to indicate their feelings: green = happy, yellow = so-so, red = sad or angry. You could use circles of these colors with the pocket chart or have students place a shape of the appropriate color on the corner of their desks. (Unifix cubes work well for this purpose.)
4. One way to take a quick "temperature check" throughout the day might be to ask the class to indicate how they are feeling at that moment by showing a thumbs up, thumbs to the side (so-so), or thumbs down. This works well for all ages.

How Do You Feel Today?

As one of the ways to check the emotional temperature of your class, I mentioned a How Do You Feel? chart. In the remainder of this chapter, I describe how to make and introduce such a chart, and how to use it as part of your daily routine.

Constructing the Pocket Chart

1. Determine how many pockets you will need; there should be one for each child, each teacher and regular classroom guest, and a couple of extras for new students. Also decide on the best orientation for the poster board, which may be determined by the space where you want to place it.
2. Cut 1 1/2" strips from one piece of the poster board to make the pockets. (Vertical strips of tape will be used to separate the strips into individual pockets.) The number of strips is determined by the number of pockets you need.
3. For 20 pockets on a sheet of 22" x 28" poster board, measure four horizontal pocket lines 5" apart, starting from the bottom of the poster board and working up. This leaves two inches at the top for attaching the chart title.
4. Next mark off five vertical lines 5" to 5 1/2" apart, forming five columns of pockets.
5. Place the poster board strips along the horizontal lines. Attach them to the poster board with the cloth tape, being sure that half of the tape is on the strip and the other half is on the poster board.
6. Place strips of cloth tape around the outside edges of the poster board to secure the ends of the pockets. Then

Objectives

- To get a sense of the overall emotional temperature of the class by looking at this chart throughout the day
- To recognize how individual students are feeling
- To take appropriate measures to calm or energize individual students or the class so everyone is in a good emotional frame to do his or her best work
- To allow students to see the emotional temperature of their class and individual peers
- To promote empathy among students as they learn to adjust their interactions to students who are feeling happy, sad, so-so, or angry
- To foster awareness of the emotional temperature of the class so everyone can interact in a more compassionate, empathetic, and respectful way

Materials

✔ 2 sheets of 22" x 28" poster board
✔ 2 rolls of colored cloth tape
✔ yardstick
✔ pencil
✔ scissors or large paper cutter
✔ laminated animal or character cutout
✔ construction paper
✔ stapler
✔ marking pens or dark crayons for each student
✔ safety scissors for each student
✔ circle template or stencil cut from poster board for each student (The plastic lid of an 11oz. coffee can makes a good template.)

place vertical strips of cloth tape along the vertical lines you have marked to divide the strips into pockets.

7. Write a name on each pocket for each member of your classroom community. To reuse the chart year after year, write the individuals' names on stickers. The stickers can be peeled off or simply covered over each year.
8. Make a title to attach to the top of the chart. I like to perch an animal or character cutout in one corner with a speech balloon that says, "How do you feel today?"
9. Staple the chart to a bulletin board at eye level on a side wall where it is easily seen.

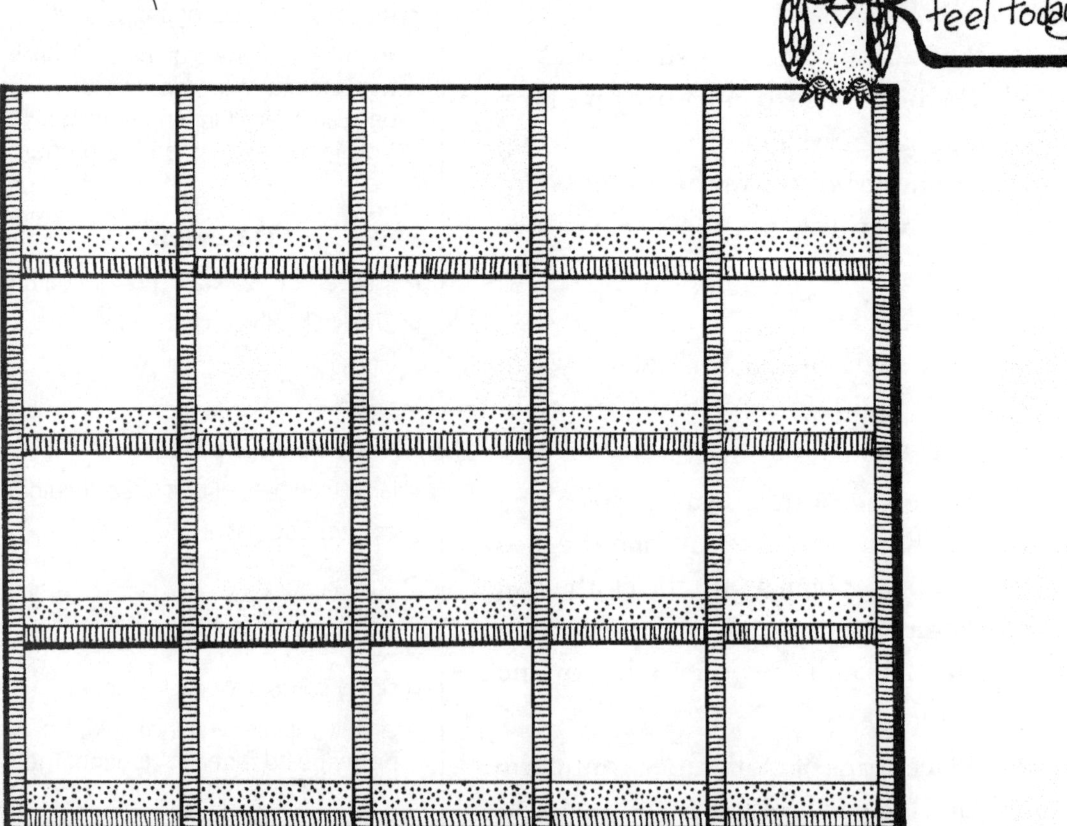

Constructing the Feeling Faces

1. Give each student a circle template or stencil and two squares of construction paper a little larger than the template.
2. Ask each student to trace a circle on each square of construction paper, then to cut out the circles.
3. Have each student draw a face on each side of the two circles to depict the following emotions: happy, sad, angry, and so-so. (Have extra materials ready for visitors or newcomers to make their own feeling faces.)
4. Have students put their faces in their respective chart pockets, being sure that the face indicating how they feel at the time is showing.

Alternative: You may prefer to have a chart with a hook for each classroom member. Laminate the faces and punch a hole in each so the student can hang it in his or her space.

Introducing the Pocket Chart

It is best to introduce the How Do You Feel Today? chart at the beginning of the school year so that it becomes an integral part of the daily routine. It is never too late to make one, however.

1. Explain that it is important for you to know how everyone in the class is feeling each day at school. Ask students why they think this is important. After discussion, explain that knowing how they all feel individually and as a group will help you know how best to work with them so they can do their best work.
2. Ask, "Why would it be helpful to each of you to know how everyone in the room is feeling?" Allow for discussion.
3. Drawing your students' attention to the How Do You Feel Today? chart on the bulletin board, explain that this chart will help all of us in the class understand how we all are feeling so that we can help each other learn, get along with one another better, and do our best work.

Using the Pocket Chart

Ask your students to think about how they feel as they come into the classroom each morning, and to place the appropriate feeling face so it shows in their pocket. Encourage them to change the face throughout the day if their mood changes.

Use the information you get about your students' feelings proactively in managing your classroom; for example, spend a few minutes with individual students who are sad or so-so, offering them a calming activity to ease them into the day. If you hold a class meeting, comment on the emotional temperature of your class. Should you notice that the class is collectively in a bad mood, you might say, "As I look at the feeling chart this morning, I notice that many of us are feeling either sad or so so-so. Let's see if we can boost our spirits by doing [suggest an activity] so that we can do our best work at school today." The time you take to do a feeling-booster activity could make the difference between a bad day and a pretty good day!

Now that you have taken the emotional temperature of your class, both individually and collectively, what can you do about it? Sample the remaining dishes on the pu pu platter of techniques in the following chapters and see which ones work best to change your students' states of being.

Chapter 9

Breathing for Relaxation

Even young children can learn deep breathing exercises. Initially, you can present a few minutes of structured belly breathing at appropriate times of day, such as before a test or when students return from recess and need to settle down to work. Once students have mastered the technique, reminders should suffice, and eventually you will begin to see them utilizing this strategy independently.

Introducing Belly Breathing

Before I begin to teach abdominal breathing, I like to explain why breathing is important and the difference between deep and shallow breathing, presenting essentially the same information you read in chapter 3. The following procedure is geared to young children. Feel free to adapt it as appropriate for the age and understanding level of your class.

Objectives

- To understand why breathing is important
- To recognize the difference between deep and shallow breathing
- To understand how deep breathing helps the body and brain work better

Materials

✔ small, round balloon
✔ pint-sized measure or pint bottle
✔ 1/2-cup measure
✔ chalkboard and chalk or white board and dry-erase markers

1. Explain that the oxygen in the air we breathe is what powers everything in our bodies: it makes the brain able to think and every other part of our bodies able to do its job.
2. Ask what happens when we breathe in. Explain that air goes into two lungs in the chest (draw the lungs on the chalkboard), which are kind of like two balloons inside us. (Show the balloon.) Encourage students to put their hands on their chests to feel their lungs filling with air as they take a deep breath. Simultaneously, you should blow up the balloon. (An alternative if you have trouble blowing up balloons would be to fill one with water.)

3. Continue by explaining that from our lungs, blood vessels take the oxygen from the air to every part of the body. Other blood vessels bring used air in the form of carbon dioxide back to the lungs after our body is finished with it. Then our lungs breathe out (or exhale) the carbon dioxide and breathe in (or inhale) new, fresh air full of oxygen.
4. Explain that babies naturally take big, deep breaths, so their bellies rise and fall with each breath. Demonstrate by taking a deep breath and blowing the balloon up completely, then letting the air out again.
5. Tell students that a lot of people forget to breathe this way as they grow older. Why? Because when we get scared or tense, our bodies tighten up and our lungs can't fill as far. Or sometimes we might wear tight clothes that make it harder to breathe. Point to the upper third of the lungs on your drawing and tell the children that over time, we get used to our bodies feeling tight and to taking shallow breaths from just the top part of our lungs.
6. Hold up the pint measure, saying, "If you take a big, full breath, here is about how much air goes into your lungs. If your body is tight and you take just a little, shallow breath, here is about how much air goes into your lungs." (Hold up the half-cup measure.)
7. Say, "Remember that our bodies need the oxygen in the air to make everything work. Do you think that our bodies will work better when we get this much air (hold up pint measure) or this much air (hold up half-cup measure)? What about our brains, will they work better with this much air (indicating pint measure) or this much air (indicating half-cup measure)?"

Learning Belly Breathing

Objectives

- To learn to do deep abdominal breathing
- To learn to use deep abdominal breathing to relax or focus

Materials

✔ chalkboard and chalk or white board and dry-erase markers
✔ balloon (optional)
✔ lightweight book for each child (optional)

1. Refer to the diagram on the chalkboard or white board and divide the lungs into thirds. In this way, your students can visualize the three parts to this breathing pattern as they practice it.
2. For younger students especially, you may want to blow up a balloon to show how the lungs inflate from the bottom up.
3. If you have carpet in your room, you might have younger students lie down on their backs as they go through the three steps to learning deep abdominal breathing.
4. Repeat the procedure given in chapter 3 for learning abdominal breathing (see page 35), having children place their hands on their bellies, then their sides, then their collarbones and upper chests, feeling the air fill each part of their lungs. Demonstrate each part of the breathing technique by having your students watch what your body does as you breathe. For example, turn sideways so that they can see your belly go out as you inhale and back in as you exhale for the first part. Then have them watch as your rib cage expands for the second part. Showing your students how *not* to breathe during Part III of the procedure (that is, in the clavicular area) helps them to see and sense what deep breathing should look like. When I do this, I exaggerate filling the top part of my lungs by stretching tall, bringing my shoulders up to my ears, and bugging my eyes out. The children can immediately see that this way of breathing is tense, not relaxed. I remind them that their shoulders should not rise, but should stay still, then show them what breathing this way looks like.

5. You will need to walk around the room to make sure that your students are placing their hands in the right places to feel what happens as they breathe. Also watch for paradoxical breathing, which is where the belly goes in instead of out on the inhalation. When they try to focus on their breathing, children may initially tense up and use this pattern.
6. For children who are learning this technique lying down, you might have each one place a book on his or her belly as a cue to taking full breaths. Can they see the book rise and fall with each breath? Students could work with a partner, each taking a turn watching while the other breathes to check whether the book rises. If you use this cue, you might refer to deep abdominal breathing as "book belly breathing."

Refer to the book *Breathwalk,* by Gurucharan Singh Khalsa, Ph.D., and Yogi Bhajan, Ph.D., to find out how using primal sounds or phonemes (the simplest speech units) can increase the effectiveness of the 4/4 and 8/8 breathing patterns.

7. Once the students understand deep belly breathing, have them set a slow breathing pattern by counting silently to four as they inhale and again as they exhale. As they become more proficient, you can have them gradually increase the count to eight for both halves of the breathing cycle.
8. Young students love animals, so using an animal name to label this breathing pattern can help cement it in their minds. In *Breathwalk,* Khalsa and Bhajan (2000) call the 4/4 or 8/8 complete breathing pattern the **Tiger Breath.** Labeling the breath in such a way gives you an easy cue to prompt deep breathing. For example, "I see that we need to get centered. Let's take a minute to do the Tiger Breath. Four counts in and four counts out."

Raisin Focusing Activity

Now that your students know how to do deep abdominal breathing, they are ready to examine what it means to be focused. We often say things such as, "Joey, you need to get focused," or "Class, we need to refocus so that we can finish this lesson." Does Joey or your class really understand what it means to be focused? Perhaps not. I believe that we need to help our students know and feel what this means. If they know what being focused feels like, they can then use the breath to help themselves get there or return there when needed.

Here is a tried-and-true activity to do just that. This experience forces students to pay attention to the process of eating a raisin, moment by moment. This feeling of total immersion in the act of eating a raisin demonstrates what being fully focused is like.

Objectives

- To experience what it is like to be fully focused on something, to be in the moment
- To list adjectives that describe a raisin (optionally as the basis of a future writing project)

Materials

- ✔ 2 raisins per child
- ✔ 1 toothpick per child
- ✔ paper cup or plate to hold raisins

1. Ask your students what it means to be really focused. Invite volunteers to describe times when they felt they were focused. Explain that you are going to help them learn what it feels like to bring their full attention to something, to be focused.
2. Explain that you will be passing around a plate (or cup) of raisins and toothpicks. Each student may take two raisins off the plate with a toothpick and pass the plate on. Once they have their raisins, students may eat one but should hold the other raisin in the palm of one hand. (If a student doesn't like raisins, perhaps you could have grapes or blueberries

available as an alternative. It is always wise to ensure that no students have food allergies or dietary restrictions that would preclude using raisins.)

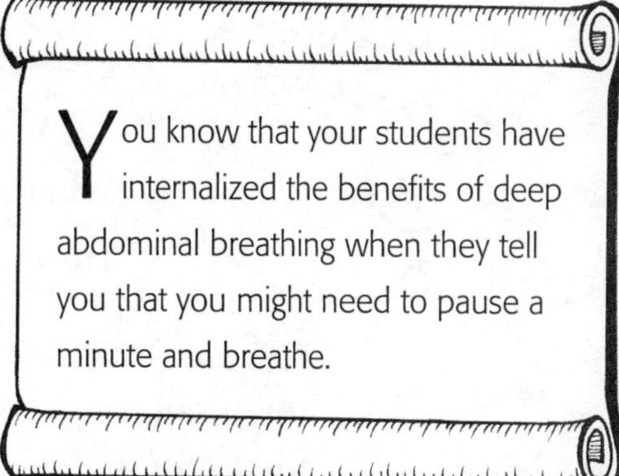

3. Encourage students just to sit with their raisins, noticing all they can about them.
4. After a few minutes, ask students to think of words that describe what their raisins look and feel like. If you like, these can be written on the board and used later for a related writing task.
5. When students have contributed all the words they can think of, tell them that when you say so, and not before, they may put their raisins into their mouths and just let them sit there without biting into them. Encourage them to notice their raisins, to feel them with their tongues. What does a raisin feel like?
6. Then tell them to take just one bite and notice what happens. After paying attention to that experience, they may chew their raisins slowly, paying attention to what is happening inside their mouths. They gradually work their raisins to the backs of their mouths and swallow them.
7. Ask your students to comment upon the experience. You may well hear comments such as:
   - *"I never paid attention to what happens when I ate a raisin before."*
   - *"I really noticed what the raisin felt like in my mouth."*
   - *"They taste better when you eat them slowly."*
8. Relate the experience of focusing on the raisins to other times when students have been completely immersed in or attending to a task, asking questions such as these:

- Can you recall a time when your attention was fully focused on something?
- What was it?
- What were you doing?
- How was that experience similar to eating the raisin?

This activity provides your students with a concrete experience to help them remember what it feels like to be focused. You may remind your students of this activity when they need to focus or refocus their attention on something at another time. Using the breath is an easy way to change your students' state of being, and when combined with simple body positions, it adds a physical benefit as well. What am I talking about? You guessed it, yoga!

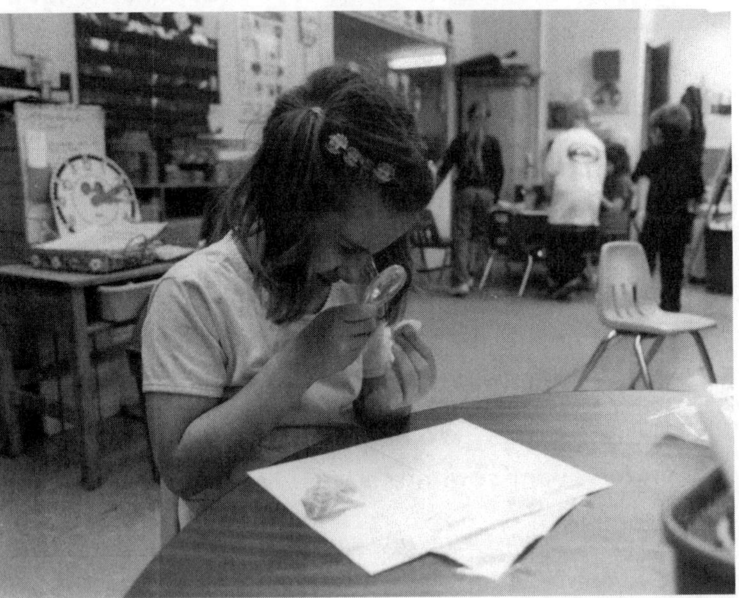

This first grader exemplifies what it looks like to be fully focused.

Chapter 10

Helping Students Relax and Revive with Yoga

The deep breathing, focused attention, and controlled movement in yoga offer students a gentle way to stretch their muscles, thus relieving tension and reaching a more relaxed state. Reducing their internal stress levels puts them in a balanced and unified state where their bodies, minds, and spirits can work together more effectively, often improving performance. You might ask students how they feel before and after doing a yoga posture or session.

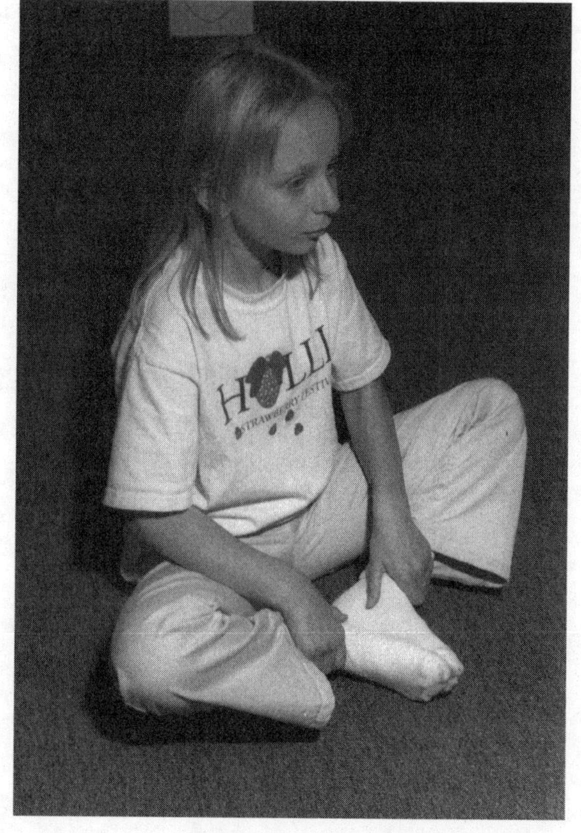

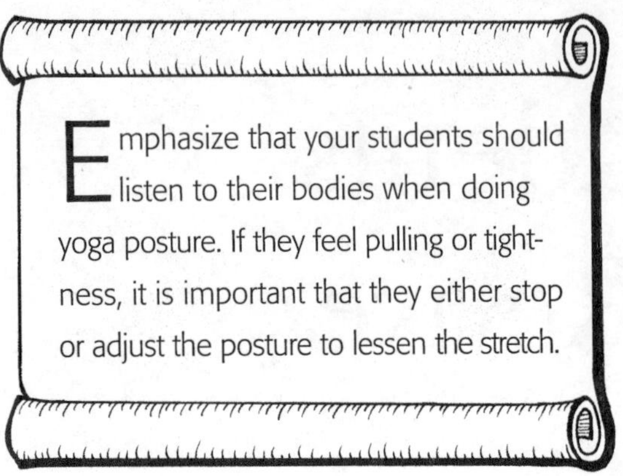

If you have a carpeted area in your classroom, this is the best place to try the following yoga postures. Should you not have a carpeted area, you might ask each student to bring in a beach towel or small rug for yoga time. Alternatively, you can use the seated versions of these postures. The seated versions may also be more appropriate for older students. Always model the postures before having students assume them.

Yoga postures are easily incorporated into centering time during your classroom meeting (more on this in chapter 11), into transition times, and whenever the need arises for individuals or the class as a whole. With young children, it is important to make doing yoga playful. Where appropriate, I offer suggestions to do just that. For them, the focus is more on body awareness than the correctness of the posture or how long it is held.

Lion Pose

This pose is helpful in releasing anger and frustration through bringing fresh oxygen to the face and throat (Lusk 1998). I describe the posture being done on the floor, but it may be done in a chair as well.

1. Have your students begin this pose by kneeling on the floor and sitting back on their heels with a straight spine and their hands resting on their knees. If kneeling is uncomfortable, they can place a rolled towel between their buttocks and calves. To help them lengthen their spines, have them imagine that they are marionettes and that the string on the crown (top) of their head is being pulled. This image will help them press the crown upward, elongating the spine.

2. As your students inhale deeply, have them make their eyes bug out, stick out their tongues, and splay their fingers out. Then have them release their breath with a lion's roar. Younger students might like to play with this posture by pouncing forward as they roar and landing on all fours.
3. Repeat this procedure a couple of times.

Child Pose

This posture relieves lower back tension and increases circulation to the belly and lower back (Sarley and Sarley 1999).

1. Have your students begin by kneeling on the floor and sitting back on their heels. Make sure that their spines are straight and their arms are at their sides with their hands resting on the floor. (Use the marionette image described in the Lion Pose to help them elongate the spine.) If they feel any strain on their knees, they may roll up their beach towel or small rug and place it between their calves and thighs. This should alleviate the pressure.
2. From this posture, students inhale deeply, and on the exhale slowly lower their chests to their knees until their foreheads touch the floor. Their arms slide along the floor beside them, with the palms remaining up.

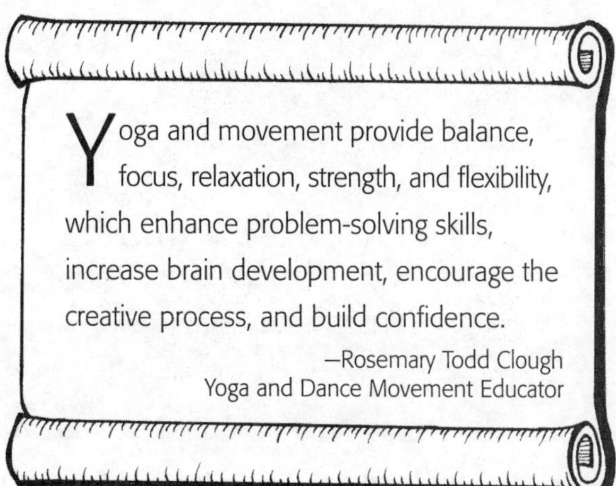

Yoga and movement provide balance, focus, relaxation, strength, and flexibility, which enhance problem-solving skills, increase brain development, encourage the creative process, and build confidence.

—Rosemary Todd Clough
Yoga and Dance Movement Educator

3. Have students hold this posture for several breaths, noticing the feeling of stretching and lengthening their spines. For a further stretch, they can bring their arms forward and rest them on the floor in front of them. If this feels like too much of a stretch, they can cross their arms, one forearm directly on top of the other, right in front of their heads. If they prefer, they can rest their heads on their crossed forearms.
4. When they feel ready to release the posture, they take one last deep breath, and on the exhale slowly return to the sitting position, straightening one vertebra at a time, starting at the tailbone. (You might have younger students feel their backbones before you start so they know what their vertebrae are.) You might say, "Come up slowly one vertebra, or back bump, at a time. End by sitting in a dignified posture, like the president would, with your arms at your sides, just like the way you started."

Note: With older students, you may prefer to do the modified child pose as described on page 51.

This boy is releasing the tension in his back by assuming the child pose.

Dog and Cat Pose

The dog and cat pose is another posture that stretches the spine, releasing tension and relaxing the body (Kent 1999).

1. Have your students begin by getting down on all fours. Their hands should be directly under their shoulders and their knees directly below their hips. Their heads should be in line with their spines and their eyes focused on the floor between their hands. Remind them to keep their shoulders relaxed throughout this stretch.
2. Have students inhale while slowly lowering their backs creating a sideways C shape running from their heads to their tails (Clough, personal communication). They end up in a swaybacked position. This is the "dog" part of the posture. Have them hold this position briefly to feel the shape of their bodies. Younger students may wish to wag their tails (bottoms) and bark like a dog.

The first part of the dog and cat pose can be described as resembling an old swaybacked horse.

3. As they exhale, they arch their backs while dropping their heads toward the floor. This is the "cat" part of the posture. Again, having students hold this position briefly helps them feel the shape of their bodies. Younger students might like to meow like a cat.

In the second part of the cat pose, this student arches his back like a cat while dropping his head toward the floor.

4. Have your students repeat this cycle several times, timing their inhalations and exhalations so they are the same length. You may want to establish a rhythm by saying, "Inhale, back down. . . . Exhale, back up."

Alternative Chair Position

This posture can be modified to be accomplished while sitting forward in a chair. Have your students move their chairs back from their desks, sit with spines straight, and rest their hands on their knees. They inhale and on the exhalation lower their heads and arch their backs. As they inhale, they raise their heads and curve their backs inward. Repeat this sequence several times.

Standing Forward Bend

Here is another useful lower back stretch.

1. Have students begin by planting their feet eight to ten inches apart, keeping their spines straight and their shoulders relaxed. Tell them to bend their knees slightly. Their arms should hang relaxed at their sides with the palms facing in.
2. Students inhale, and on the exhale slowly bend their bodies at the hips, allowing their arms to dangle in front of them. Remind them to keep their knees slightly bent with their torsos as close to their thighs as possible. You can describe this posture as imitating a limp Raggedy Ann or Raggedy Andy rag doll. Some of my first graders likened it to "hangin' like a monkey."
3. While in the rag-doll position, students take long, deep breaths. They may give a loud sigh, "ahhhhh," on each exhalation, to further release tension from their bodies. Demonstrate this for them and have them join in.
4. After several deep breaths, tell students to take one last deep breath in, and on the exhalation, rise slowly, one vertebra (or back bump) at a time, starting at the tailbone. (Again, you may wish to have younger students feel their backs before they start.) Have your students hold this relaxed standing position for a few moments.

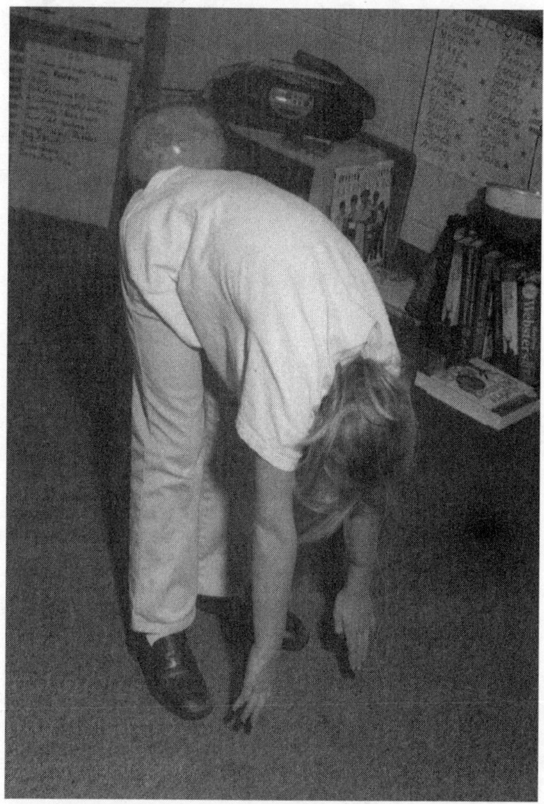

The standing forward bend looks like a limp rag doll.

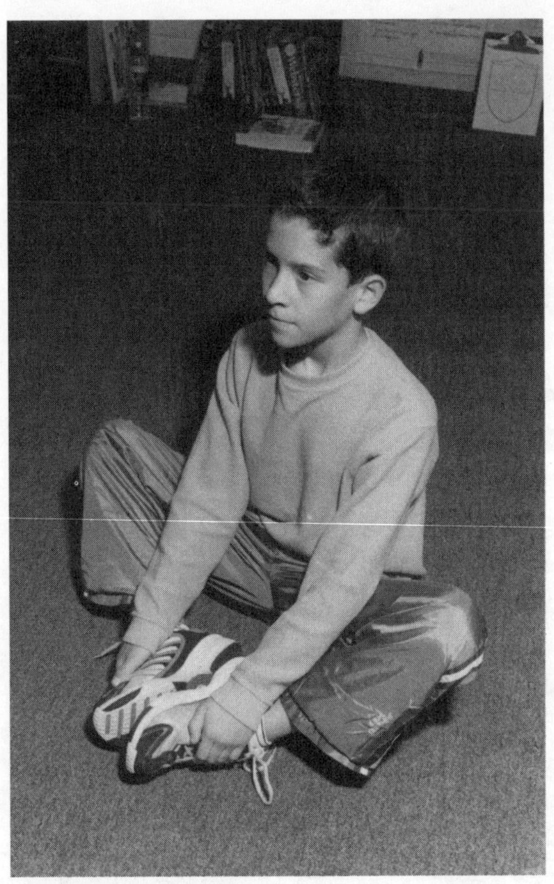

Doing yoga helps this boy return to his work in a more balanced and focused state.

Another benefit of doing yoga with your students is that it reinforces the idea of being focused. Through yoga, they learn to center their attention and breathing on holding each posture briefly. Having focused on that one posture for a few moments, they can take that focus with them into their work. Other centering techniques are addressed in chapter 11.

Chapter 11

Centering

Centering is an effective way to help students become still, more relaxed, and better able to focus their attention where it needs to be. Learning to center involves a quieting process for bringing their awareness from their minds to the gravitational center of their bodies, or their heart centers. Doing this clears and relaxes the mind and body so they function better, which translates into better classroom performance. Initially, your students may giggle or feel self-conscious during centering activities. As they learn and experience the effects of stillness and how it can help them to focus, however, the giggles will cease. With persistence, you and your students will see the benefits.

Some of the centering and visualization activities described in this chapter are done with eyes closed, so throughout the chapter I refer to having students close their eyes. I suggest you offer this as a choice and do not require that students close their eyes. If any parents object to visualization for religious or other reasons, you may offer a choice of a quiet activity, such as silent reading, or simply have the child sit quietly with the rest of the class during the activity, so as not to draw attention to his or her nonparticipation.

Finding Your Center

Finding Your Center is a good activity for class meeting time. My preference is to have the class stand in a circle while learning this technique. Older students may prefer to stand behind their desks, however, so they feel less conspicuous. This type of centering can be done while sitting in a chair, once your students have experienced the first standing exploration. Their feet should be planted firmly on the floor.

1. Begin by explaining that students are going to learn to do something called **centering** that will help them to be more relaxed and focused in school or when doing other activities that require concentration.
2. Ask your students to stand with their feet planted firmly on the floor, a little less than shoulder width apart, with arms relaxed and hanging loosely at their sides. Have students take three deep abdominal breaths, then close their eyes. They should stand like this breathing normally for a few breaths.
3. Now ask them to bring their attention into their minds. Pause for a few moments, then have them open their eyes and share what they noticed, asking

   - Did you feel stable? Unstable?
   - Did you become still inside, or was your mind still busy?

4. Most likely your students will report that they felt a bit unstable and their minds were not still. Explain that they are going to learn a technique that will help them become still inside and more stable at the same time. This technique will help them relax so they can do a better job at school or wherever they may be.
5. Next, ask your students to imagine that there is a tiny elevator that runs all the way up from their tailbones to the top of their heads where their minds are. Say, "We are going to take a ride on this tiny elevator today from our tailbones up to our minds and then down to our bellies." (Expect a few giggles.) You might prefer to use the phrase *lower abdomen* with older students.
6. First students must know exactly where you mean when you say **belly** or **lower abdomen.** Place your hands just below your waistline and ask them to do the same, saying, "This is where our elevator ride will take us, up from our tailbones to our minds, then down to our bellies." (Younger students might touch their tailbones, the tops of their heads, and their bellies.)
7. Just as before, have your students plant their feet firmly on the floor, arms relaxed at their sides, and take three deep breaths. Then have them shut their eyes. After a few normal breaths, have them imagine themselves stepping into the tiny elevators at their tailbones and, as they inhale, riding it up to the top floor, their minds. Then, as they exhale, have them imagine riding the elevator down to their bellies. Tell them to stay here, bringing their attention into their bellies. After a minute or so, have them imagine themselves getting off the tiny elevator. (You may lengthen the time they focus on their bellies as they get used to the activity.) They may now open their eyes.

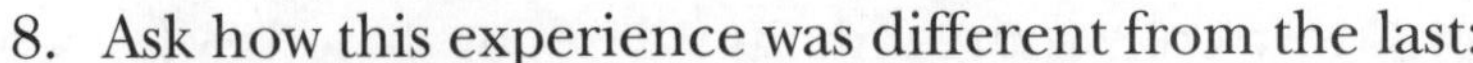

8. Ask how this experience was different from the last:
   - What did you notice?
   - Did being in your belly feel the same as being in your mind? Different?
   - When did you feel most stable: when you were in your mind or in your belly?

9. Repeat this exercise and again ask your students whether they are more stable when they stand with their attention in their minds or in their bellies. Take a quick survey. You might demonstrate the increased stability of being centered by inviting a volunteer to stand in the center of the circle. First have the student focus in his or her mind. Then push gently on the shoulders, and the student will wobble. Next have the student focus attention into his or her belly while you gently push again. With a centered focus, the student will be more stable.

   Note: If time is short, you may break the lesson here. If possible, continue it the next day (or later the same day), so students do not forget the feeling of being centered.

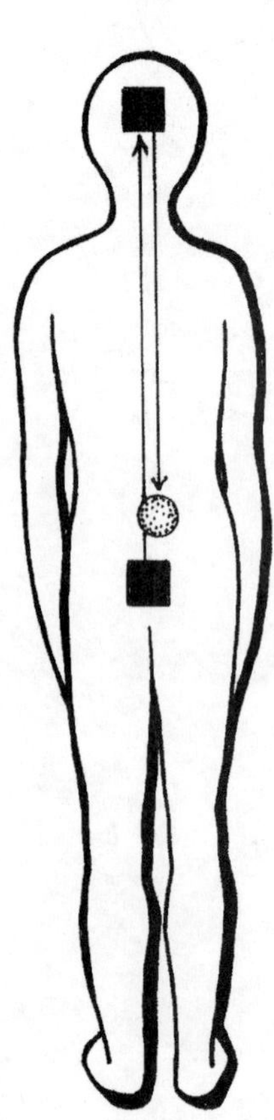

10. Have your students take the elevators down to their bellies again, following the same procedure, then test each child by gently pushing on his or her shoulders. You will quickly see who has been able to reach this place of stillness and stability.

Use this technique with your students as a group whenever you see that they need grounding. With individuals, just cue them when needed by saying, for example, "Joey, elevator." Centering is a tool that your students can learn to use whenever they need to calm down due to overactivity or anxiety, or when they need sustained attention for a lengthy period, such as in a testing situation.

Centering Sessions

In my classroom, a centering session became a part of our morning classroom meeting ritual. Centering became a valued and highly anticipated part of our day. If for some reason we were not able to start the day with our classroom meeting and centering time, my third graders would often say, "But aren't we going to center today?" So, of course, we found another time to center; I looked forward to it as much as they did!

Objectives

- To learn to reach a place of calm and stillness
- To experience deep relaxation and improve focusing abilities

Materials

✔ calming, yin music (see Resource List or chapter 13 for suggestions)

✔ object from nature (such as cut flowers, a potted plant, a shell, leaves, a small terrarium, a goldfish bowl, a pumpkin, a basket of apples, or an interesting rock), a student-chosen object, or an object related to a current topic of study

Besides Finding Your Center, there are other options for centering. A typical centering session would have the following structure.

1. Begin by inviting students to sit cross-legged in a circle on the floor. (Older students may prefer to sit in chairs.) I offer students a choice of ways to hold their hands:
   - palms down on their knees
   - palms up on their knees
2. Once students are situated, turn on calming music, such as a baroque or New Age piece.
3. Place an object from nature in the middle of the circle. Everyone (including you) takes a few deep belly breaths with eyes open or closed. Then all cast their eyes on the object.

4. When you are ready to end the session, invite your students to remove their gaze from the object in the middle of the circle, to close their eyes, and to picture the object in their mind's eye. Then invite your students to slowly bring their awareness back to the classroom by turning their heads from side to side, wiggling their fingers and toes, and then opening their eyes again as you fade out the music. You may wish to discuss the students' experiences before moving on.

A vase of gladioli is the focus of this centering session.

Variations on the Centering Session

Instead of using an object from nature, you might invite a student of the week to bring in a prized possession to be placed in the middle of the circle. Another option is to use an object related to a topic your class is studying as the focal point. You might also have all of the students silently draw the object in the middle of the circle while the music plays.

Instead of sitting in a circle, you could have students find a comfortable position either sitting or lying on the floor, turn on the music, and do any of the following:

- Read a poem or poems.
- Do a guided visualization. (I provide several guided visualizations beginning on page 95; many books and audiotapes of guided visualizations are also commercially available.)
- Take your students through deep belly breathing.
- Have your students lie on their backs. Guide them through focusing on and relaxing one part of the body at a time.
- Let each student finger-walk a spiral or Cretan labyrinth (described beginning on page 102).
- Do a yoga posture or postures (see chapter 10).
- Have your students focus their attention on an affirmation (described beginning on page 115).
- Have your students place their hands over their hearts (an effective technique for quieting the emotions). They might choose to send a wish or a greeting, such as a birthday greeting or get-well wish, to a classmate while in this position.

Initially, I often specify that students are either to sit or to lie down, so they have opportunities to experience each position and how it feels to them. With experience, I allow individual students to choose whichever position is most comfortable for them, unless the structure of a particular activity lends itself better to one position or the other.

There are many opportunities for you to be creative in these sessions. Try different ideas and see how they work. Each group of students is unique, and what works wonderfully with one group may not be nearly so effective with another.

Guided Visualizations

Taking your students on a guided visualization is a centering activity that helps to create balance and calmness. The possible topics for a visualization are limitless. I give several examples here, and countless others are commercially available. With experience, you may even begin creating your own guided visualizations, perhaps related to a topic your students are studying. For example, if you are studying flowers in science, create a visualization related to flowers, perhaps a journey through a flower garden where each student finds a special flower and spends some time with it, feeling and noticing its beauty.

> There are many pathways to initiating the relaxation response, but yoga, meditation, and breath work are the most facile for a classroom setting.
>
> —Susan Frey, *The Road to Avalon II* (p. 109)

How long you spend on a visualization experience will depend upon your students. As you work with centering activities, you will begin to have an inner sense of how long is long enough. You certainly do not want your students to develop negative associations with visualization and centering. It is better to err on the side of spending too little time rather than too much.

Begin a visualization by having your students lie on their backs, sit cross-legged on the floor, or sit in a chair in a dignified position. For younger students, discussing the word *dignified* might be necessary. You might relate it to how the president of the United States would sit. Another analogy would be to have your students think of themselves as human marionettes. They could imagine that there is a string attached to the tops of their heads and someone is gently pulling on it, straightening their backbones and lining up the head, neck, and spine. If you choose to have your students sit in a chair, their feet should be flat on the floor and their backs straight, not leaning back against the chair. If you have a carpeted area in your room, younger students especially may prefer to stretch out on their backs. If so, suggest that they bend their knees and place their feet flat on the floor, to prevent back strain. They may have their arms at their sides or crossed over their bellies, whichever is most comfortable.

Invite students to close their eyes as you turn on quiet, soothing music, then begin to read. Use a soft, fluid, rhythmic voice much like you would for reading poetry. The rhythm of the music you choose to play during the visualization usually dictates the pace of your reading, but generally your pace should feel relaxed not hurried. Pause frequently to give students time to fully experience the images in their minds, to be in each moment. The ellipses in the following visualizations represent suggested places to pause.

Objectives

- To experience being centered, balanced, and calm
- To empower students to self-calm whenever needed
- To provide a springboard for extension art or writing activities (optional)

Materials

✔ quiet (yin) music (see Resource List)
✔ text or tape for guided visualization

Forest Walk Visualization

Feel free to adjust the wording of the following visualization as appropriate for your grade level. If you do not have pine forests in your region of the country, feel free to alter the description of the forest to suit your locale.

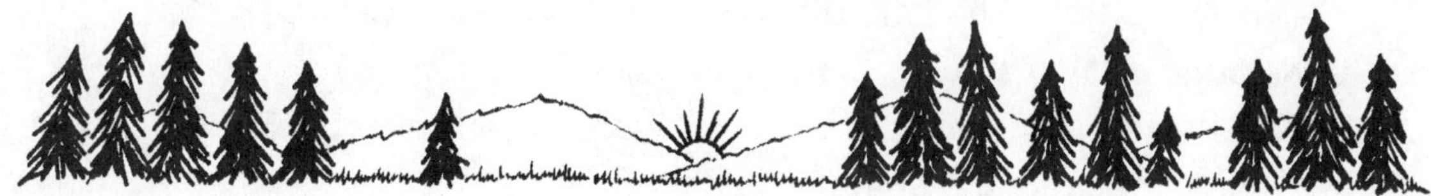

Today we are going to take a walk in a forest of tall pine trees. Each of you will find a special tree there, a tree that you can call your own . . . one that you can return to any time you wish . . . a tree that will offer you a safe place to rest . . . a safe place to be . . . a place where you can go when you feel happy . . . sad . . . angry . . . or just want to be alone . . . If you should find your tree before the rest of us, just be with it until we find ours.

Let's begin our walk . . . The pine forest begins at the edge of a great meadow of tall grasses, black-eyed Susans, and milkweed pods. As you step into the forest, a coolness greets you . . . You walk silently upon a path of soft pine needles . . . You follow the path . . . looking to your right . . . looking to your left . . . looking ahead . . . searching for the perfect tree . . . the tree you can call your own. **[Pause for a few moments to allow students to search for their trees.]** And, when you see your tree . . . go over to it . . . touch it, feel the bark . . . smell it . . . hug it . . . This is your special tree. . .

Now, sit beneath it and lean your back against it. . . . Notice its strength . . . Be with your tree . . . How do you feel when you are resting against it? . . . Just be with it. . . . Be one with your tree. . . . Appreciate its size . . . its shape . . . its strength . . . its willingness to support you . . . to be there for you . . . **[long pause]**

And now, it is time to leave your special tree . . . your special friend . . . Give your tree a good-bye hug. . . . Thank it for being there for you . . . for supporting you . . . You know that it will always be there for you . . . And now . . . walk quietly . . . silently . . . along the soft path of pine needles . . . back to the edge of the forest . . . Walk out of the pine forest . . . into the great meadow . . . with gratitude in your heart for the gift of peace and comfort it has given you.

And, when you are ready . . . you may return to our classroom by turning your head from side to side, shrugging your shoulders a few times, wiggling your fingers, wiggling your toes, and opening your eyes, if they are closed. Know that you can always return to your special tree whenever you wish . . . wherever you are.

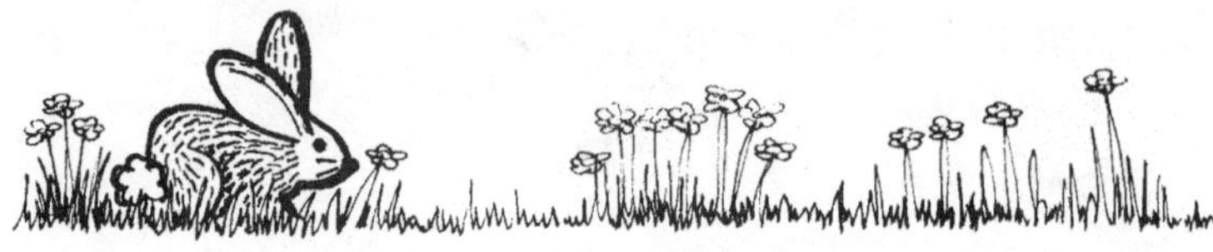

Hot-Air Balloon Visualization

Today, we are going to take an imaginary hot-air balloon ride . . . We begin our trip by walking to a large field where a hot-air balloon sits waiting for each of you. See the balloon ahead of you . . . What color is it? . . . Does it have a design on it? . . . If it is striped, what colors are the stripes? . . . Now, climb into the basket of the balloon. You're safely inside and ready to take off . . . What are you feeling as you wait for liftoff?

Before you know it, the burner has been lit . . . The ropes are released . . . and up you go . . . up into the sky . . . up, up, up . . . higher, and higher, and higher . . . sailing across the sky on the breath of a light breeze. . . . What do you see as you look down? . . . What do you see as you look around you? . . . How do you feel being up so high? . . . You are drifting, drifting across our state of ______ **[name of your state]** . . . and across other states in our country **[You may name some.]** . . . on, and on, and on . . . across the ______ Ocean **[Name the nearest ocean.]** . . . across the countries of ______ **[Name appropriate countries.]**, and the continents of _______ **[name them]**.

. . . As you sail across the sky, send a loving message from your heart to all the people and creatures below. . . . Let your heart radiate a message of peace . . . of hope . . . of kindness . . . of love and connectedness to all the peoples of the world . . . and to all the creatures of the world . . . **[long pause]**

And now, your hot-air balloon has circled the earth and is returning to the field where it was launched . . . It is slowly beginning to descend . . . The launch field is in sight below . . . With a soft bump, bump, bump, you land . . . Your trip is over . . . Quietly, you climb out of the hot-air balloon and walk back to school . . . back to our classroom . . . What a wonderful, heartfelt journey it has been!

Slowly turn your head from one side to the other . . . Shrug your shoulders a few times . . . Circle your wrists in one direction . . . and then the other . . . Wiggle your toes. And finally, open your eyes, if they are closed . . . You will be back in our classroom at _____ School **[name of your school].**

Rocky Coast Visualization

Pachelbel Canon with Ocean Sounds (see Resource List) or some other music with ocean sounds is particularly apropos for this visualization. Again, feel free to adjust the descriptions to fit your locale and experiences your students are likely to have had.

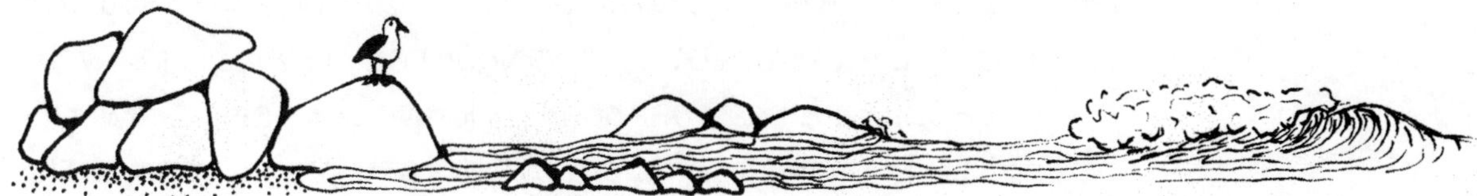

Today we will visit the rocky seacoast of the North Atlantic. . . . Each of us will find a special rock to sit upon as we watch the waves roll in to shore. . . . Let's begin by walking toward the rocky coast. As you near the ocean, notice the smell of the salty air . . . and the squawking of the seagulls flying overhead. . . . You take a deep breath and look out toward the ocean. . . . Sunlight sparkles on the waves as they roll in. . . . The water lapping against the field of rocks below creates a soothing rhythm. . . . Already you feel calmer . . . connected to nature through the song of the sea. . . .

Now, glance around at the field of rocks before you. . . . There are large boulders near the edge of the beach where you stand. . . . Farther down, you can see smaller boulders covered with blue green algae. . . . And as you look toward the water's edge, you see smaller and smaller rocks. . . . They are covered with seaweed . . . with rockweed . . . and farther down, a stringy seaweed called knotted wrack. . . . You begin to walk, moving from one boulder to the next . . . looking for the best place to sit, to just be. . . .

Finally, you find your special sitting rock. . . . Is it one of the large boulders? . . . Is it one of the rocks covered with blue green algae? . . . Or is it one of the seaweed-covered rocks down by the water's edge? . . . Whatever kind of rock you have chosen, find a comfortable sitting position. . . . Watch the waves roll in. . . . Listen to the rhythmic sound of the sea. . . . Watch the seagulls gather on the water. . . . Notice the dark black cormorants standing on the rocks, drying their outstretched wings. . . . If you are near the water, notice the mollusks: periwinkles, dog whelks, and limpets. . . . Take in the sights and smells of the rocky coast. . . . Let your body relax. . . . Let your emotions calm. . . . Feel your connection to the sea. . . . Feel the strength and stability of the rock beneath you. It has weathered many a wave but it is still strong. . . . **[long pause]**

And now, it is time to leave the rocky coast for now . . . remembering that you can come back here any time you want. . . . Take a deep breath as you look around one last time. . . . Feel gratitude for the gifts the rocky seacoast has given you . . . the strength and stability of the rocks . . . the rhythmic song of the sea. . . . And as you slowly, carefully walk back over the boulders, both small and large . . . bring the peace and calm that you felt here with you as you return to our classroom.

Slowly turn your head from one side to the other. . . . Shrug your shoulders a few times. . . . Circle your wrists in one direction and then the other. Wiggle your toes. . . . And finally, open your eyes, if they are closed, ready to go on with your day.

Follow-Up

After a visualization experience, it is important to emphasize that your students can, on their own, return to the peace and comfort of this inner space. This knowledge gives them personal power to calm their emotions on their own, without adult assistance. We hope that the benefits of this practice will become part of each student's self-care kit into adulthood.

Discussing what students saw and felt during the visualization is useful. For one, your students will enjoy sharing their experiences. Second, discussion can serve to assist those who may have had difficulty visualizing see more vivid images on their next guided visualization.

Extensions

Art

An art extension might be to have your students draw pictures based on the visualization. For example, they might draw their special tree or their adventures while seeking and spending time with it. They might draw themselves floating over their homes in their hot-air balloons. Or they might draw themselves sitting on their special rock at the seashore.

Writing

Use the visualization as the basis of a creative writing or poetry assignment. You could make a class book of all the stories or poems related to a particular visualization, perhaps with illustrations, then place it in your reading corner and give each child a copy to take home.

Spirals or Labyrinths

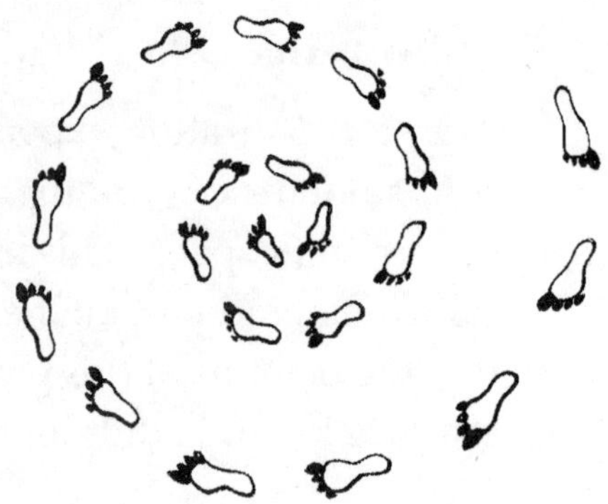

The spiral, a continuous path that circles in toward the center, is an archetypal symbol representing growth and transformation that has been present in most cultures throughout the ages. The labyrinth, too, spirals to the center and then out again, representing the same theme. As you walk through either a spiral or a labyrinth, you are forced to slow down and focus on the path to the center. This focus helps you shed your thoughts and feelings and just be in the moment, step by step, as you circle toward the center. It is through this journey to the center that transformation takes place. You move from chaos to calm and bring that new state of being with you as you circle out again. Once out, you can function in a calmer, more productive way.

In a classroom, students can get the same benefit by "walking" their fingers around a spiral or labyrinth printed on a sheet of paper. (See page 104 for a spiral and page 105 for a labyrinth; both may be reproduced for classroom use.) This tool is easily stored in a desk or notebook and provides an unobtrusive way to help students move through emotions that may be interfering with their doing their best work. It has proven to be a useful tool for first graders I have worked with at Hollis Primary School in Hollis, New Hampshire. Their teacher indicated that she encouraged her first graders to use their spirals during transition times, such as while waiting to get ready for lunch or school dismissal. She observed students who were easily distracted by sounds and movement using their spirals throughout the day, and the focused, self-directed students used their spirals without teacher direction.

Some of the first graders used their spirals at home as well. This is significant because it shows their ability to transfer this calming tool to another environment. Children who didn't have their spirals at home drew one in the air, on a rug or blanket, or on a piece of paper. The important point to note is that these young children found the spiral to be a tool they could use to change their emotional states. They learned that they could take care of themselves without outside help wherever they were. For them, the spiral was becoming a lifetime tool.

This calming and refocusing tool has been used in second-, third-, fourth-, and sixth-grade classes as well. Second graders found it very useful for calming their performance jitters. Third graders used the spiral during the mandatory state testing process to reduce their test anxiety. Half of the fourth-grade class indicated that they used it to calm their nervousness prior to tests, especially in math and spelling. Others reported using it when they were worried or frustrated. One boy mentioned that he was getting loud so he refocused himself with it.

Classroom teachers were not the only ones who tried using the spiral or labyrinth with their students. The school nurse at Hollis Primary School taped one to the wall in her office and had some of her young patients finger-walk it to calm themselves. She was amazed at how their crying quieted! A special education teacher found it very useful with students who displayed anxiety and anger management issues. One of her students with test anxiety would resume "an easy, calm flow of breathing" and could "return to the task in a more calm and focused manner" after finger-walking her spiral. This particular student would follow up her finger-walk with positive self-talk such as, "I can do this!"

When first graders at Hollis Elementary School were asked when they used the spiral and how it helped them, here are some of the answers they gave:

- *I was scared about having my tonsils out, so I used it and I wasn't scared anymore.*
- *My mom and dad were away, and I missed them. So I did the spiral and I felt better.*
- *I used it when I was tired, and I didn't feel so tired.*
- *I had a headache, and I used the spiral and my head felt better.*
- *I felt like I was going to cry, so I used the spiral and I didn't cry.*

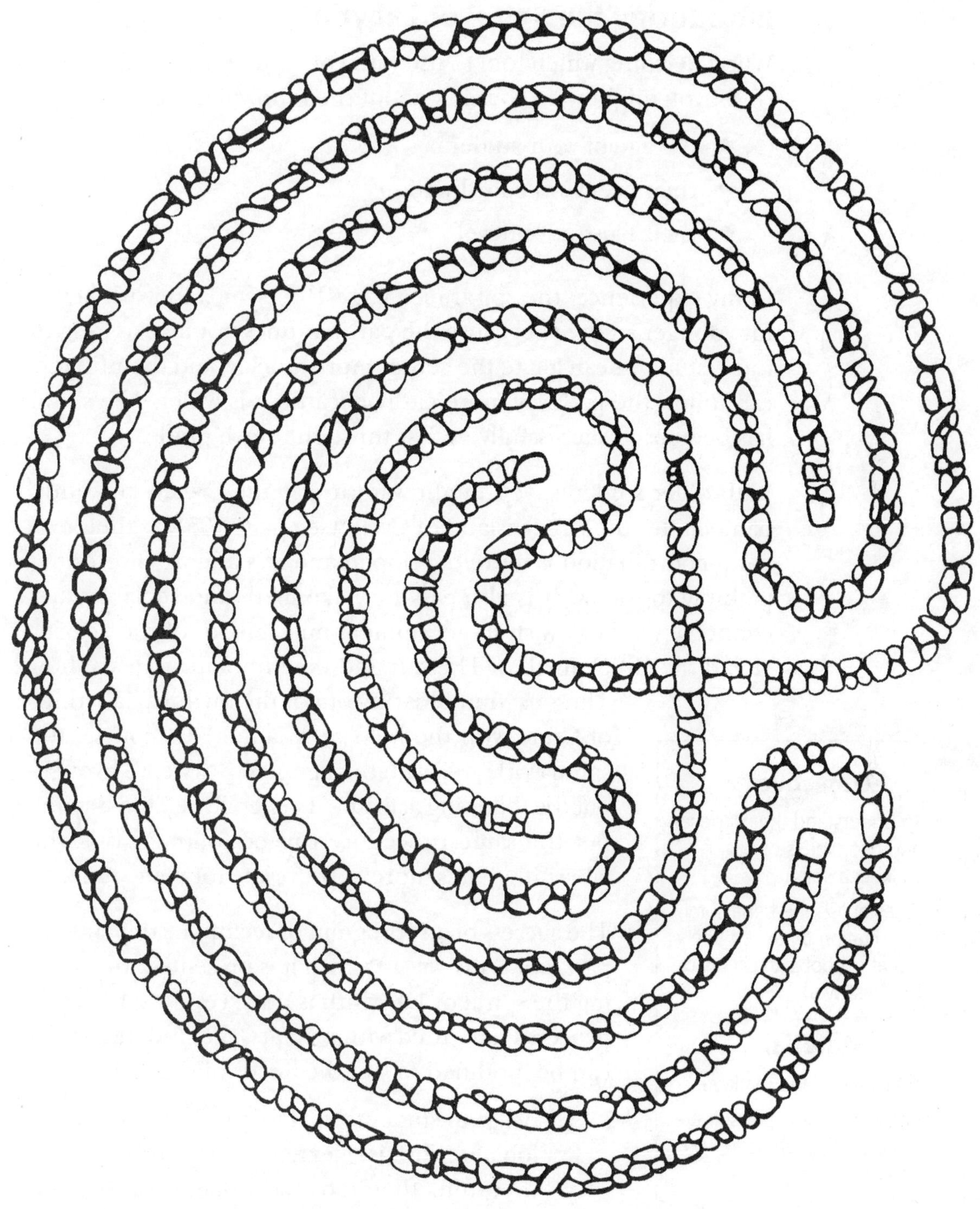

Introducing the Spiral or Labyrinth

When deciding which tool to use with your students, spiral or labyrinth, you might want to think about the following:

- the age of your students
- their eye-hand coordination
- their frustration level

In my experience, the spiral (see page 104) seems to work better for younger students because the pathway does not take as long to trace, students can get to the center more quickly, and their fingers can follow the pathway more easily because it is wider. The spiral has been used successfully in first through fourth grades.

With older students, you might want to use the Cretan labyrinth, named after the Greek island of Crete (see page 105), as their eye-hand coordination is more developed and it is a more interesting pathway to follow. It is also easy to make math and social studies connections if you wish to get optimal mileage out of the activity. (Read the Greek myth of Theseus and the Minotaur to learn how Theseus found his way out of the mythical labyrinth of Crete with the help of Ariadne.) Of course, the spiral works well with this age group as well. Throughout the following activities, I generally refer to a spiral, but the same procedure can be followed with the labyrinth, if it is more appropriate for your students.

Objectives

- To understand the purpose and usefulness of finger-walking a spiral
- To establish the behavioral expectation that everyone's job at school is to do his or her best work

Materials

- ✔ chart paper and markers
- ✔ photocopy of paper spiral or labyrinth (see page 104 or 105)
- ✔ (optional) photo of spiral petroglyphs (see Resource List)

The success of any program or technique depends, in part, upon the way in which it is presented. Introducing the spiral or labyrinth is no exception. Here is a process I have used with primary-age students which can be modified to suit the needs of older students.

1. Ask your students what they think the teacher's job at school is. Next, ask your students what they think their job at school is. All answers to both questions are acceptable. The point you want to make is that both teachers and students are there to do their best work.

2. Now ask if there are times in school when it is difficult for your students to do their best work. You will certainly hear a big "yes!"
3. Ask students to name some of the feelings or situations they have experienced that can get in the way of doing their best work. List their answers on chart paper so you can refer to them later if needed. The concerns of our students are very real and can easily interfere with their ability to focus and do their best work. You may well hear stories like these:

    ☛ *"I was worried when my friend got hurt, and I didn't get to see her because she was in another room at school."*

    ☛ *"I was mad at my brother for wrecking my building before I came to school."*

    ☛ *"I feel sad because my dad had to go on a trip, and he won't be back for a week."*

4. Ask your students if any of them has ever heard their teacher say that they need to settle down. Typically, at least a few students will raise their hands.
5. Explain that you are going to give your students another tool, the spiral, that they can use to help them feel better or calm down. This tool will help them focus their attention more fully on their schoolwork when their feelings or behaviors are getting in the way of doing their best work.
6. Hold up a paper spiral and explain that the spiral is an ancient symbol that has been found in many cultures, including the Native Americans of the Southwest. (For a learning tie-in, you could show photos of spiral petroglyphs, a common feature of southwestern Native rock art.) Continue by explaining that the spiral represents growth and transformation, which is what it will do for students as they finger-walk to the center and out again. Finger-walking a spiral can help them change their emotions to a more positive state so that they can work better in school.

Personalizing the Spiral or Labyrinth

Personalizing a paper spiral or labyrinth helps each student create a special connection to and sense of ownership of it. One first-grade teacher commented, "When students are encouraged to illustrate their spirals, powerful, intimate connections are constructed." (This is true for the teacher as well.)

Objectives

- To personalize the spirals with individualized decorations
- To learn to finger-walk the spiral as a tool for calming and self-focusing
- To transfer finger-walking the spiral to a variety of anxiety-provoking situations

Materials

✔ one copy of the paper spiral (or labyrinth) for each student (see page 104 or 105), preferably on a soft, neutral color of paper

✔ age-appropriate art materials, such as crayons or colored pencils

✔ chart paper and markers

✔ soft, flowing music such as *The Pleiades,* by Gerald Markoe (see Resource List)

1. Pass out a spiral (or labyrinth) to each student. Explain that students will be able to personalize and decorate their spirals in a special way to make them their own. They will be going through a process to do this and must listen carefully.
2. Because it is hard to resist exploring something new, allow your students to finger-walk the spiral a few times before beginning the decorating process. Have them walk their fingers between the pebbly walls.
3. Establish the parameters within which students may draw, depending on their age and level of eye-hand coordination:

   For younger children (K–2): You might want to limit the space that students can decorate so they do not color over the spiral, obscuring the pathway. For this reason, I prefer crayons and colored pencils over markers because they are lighter. Demonstrate how to fold down the corners of the paper to make triangular flaps and assist students in folding their papers. Once the corners are folded out again, tell students that they can color anywhere within the flap area. Highlighting the crease with pencil or crayon will help them to stay within the designated space. This part of the experience also provides an opportunity to casually review the geometry of rectangles, triangles, sides, corners, and points.

With younger children, have them fold down the corners of their paper spiral and decorate only the triangles outside the folds. This ensures that they will not deface or obscure the spiral.

For older students: You may allow older students to decorate around the perimeter of the spiral and even color inside it. Encourage them to use light-colored crayons or pencils, especially inside the spiral, so the pathway remains clearly discernible.

4. Explain the process to your students before they do it, so they have a sense of what is going to happen and what your behavioral expectations are.

   ☛ Students are going to listen to soft, flowing music while you guide them in personalizing their spirals. (The music helps to set the calming intention of the spiral.)

   ☛ You will ask them to close their eyes, but they don't have to if they would prefer not to. Then they will put their left hands (the receiving hand) over their hearts and their right hands (the giving hand) in the middle of their spirals.

   ☛ They will feel their heartbeats and let the rhythm flow from their hearts into their left hands, up their left arms, across their shoulders to the other arm, down that arm, through the center of their right hands, and into the center of their spirals, filling them up like pouring water from a pitcher into a glass. They should notice any colors, shapes, objects, or words that come into their mind's eye as they fill up the spiral with their heartbeats. These colors or images may be used to decorate their spirals (West 2000).

   ☛ Whenever they feel that their spirals are full of their heart songs, they may begin decorating the designated areas of the paper in silence. If they should finish decorating before others are finished, they may quietly finger-walk their spirals or do a quiet activity such as silent reading, if they get tired of finger-walking.

5. Answer any questions, then turn off the lights, turn on quiet music, ask students to place their left hands over their hearts and their right hands in the center of their spirals, and invite them to close their eyes if they choose. Tell them to take some slow, deep belly breaths, noticing the breath as they inhale and as they exhale:

Personalizing their spirals gives students a special connection to them, which increases the spirals' effectiveness as a quieting or refocusing tool. Some practitioners (for example, West 2000) advocate putting the non-dominant hand in the center of the spiral, as pictured here.

"Feel the breath as it goes in and out, in and out. Feel your bellies expand as you breathe in and collapse as you breathe out. . . . Now, notice the sound of your heartbeat, your heart song. . . . Feel the rhythm that it makes. . . . Be one with your heartbeat, the rhythm that keeps you alive. . . . Now, let your heartbeat begin to travel into your left hand, the hand that is over your heart. . . . Feel your heart beating and traveling through your hand . . . through your arm . . . like a flowing stream. . . . It travels up to your shoulder . . . across your body . . . to your other shoulder. . . . Let the rhythm of your heart song travel down your other arm . . . and flow into your right hand, which is in the middle of the spiral. . . . Feel your heartbeat flow into the center of your spiral . . . just like a stream flows into a pond and fills it up. . . . Feel your spiral fill up with the essence of you . . . your own heartbeat . . . your own life rhythm.

"What has your mind's eye noticed as your heartbeat has been flowing into the spiral? . . . Colors . . . shapes . . . designs . . . objects . . . words? . . . Be with these colors or images. . . . Be with your heart song. . . . And when your spiral feels full . . . without speaking . . . open your eyes, if they are closed, and begin to decorate your spiral paper [or the corners of your spiral paper] with the colors or images you saw in your mind's eye."

6. As students finish their visualizations, let them begin decorating their spirals with the colors, shapes, objects, or words that came to them during the experience. If any students did not get a visual image, they may decorate the spiral however they wish. Continue playing the music to maintain a sense of calmness.
7. When everyone has finished decorating, have all the students go to an open area of your room and stand in a circle with their spirals. Ask them to place their decorated spirals on the floor in front of their feet so everyone can view them in silence.
8. Have everyone turn so his or her right shoulder is facing into the circle. Let your students walk quietly around the circle to the sound of the music, looking at each spiral. When they get back to their own spiral, they may sit down.
9. If you wish, briefly discuss what students noticed during the personalizing experience and about each other's spirals.

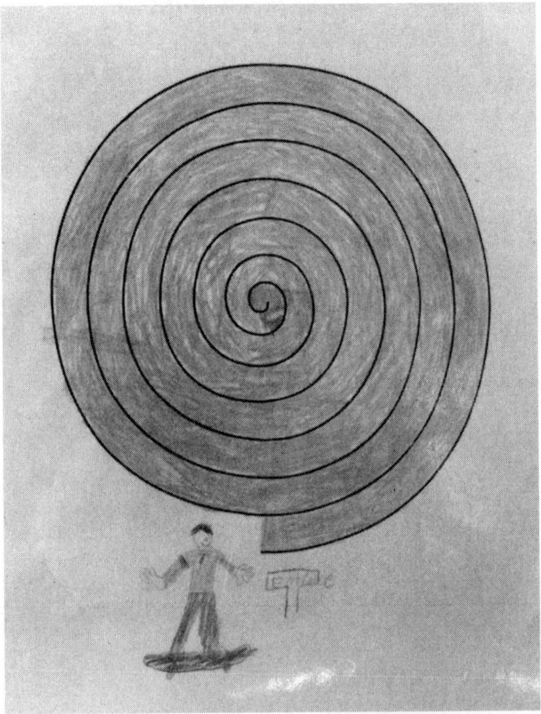

One student drew himself on a skateboard about to enter his spiral.

10. Conclude with a review of the times when students might find their spirals useful, then have everyone finger-walk their spirals once more. Ask about the experience:
    - How did you feel before finger-walking the spiral?
    - How did you feel while finger-walking the spiral?
    - How did you feel after finger-walking the spiral?

11. Record your students' thoughts on chart paper. You can refer to their comments later to remind them how finger-walking helped to change the way they were feeling. This will help them to recognize when their spirals might be useful to them in the future.

Classroom meeting time is a great time to have everyone finger-walk their spirals or labyrinths together. This is an effective way to quiet down students when they first arrive or just before they leave the meeting and go back to their desks to begin their work.

On occasion, a student may feel dizzy or even get a headache from finger-walking a spiral, perhaps from going too fast through the spiral. Suggest that the student slow down. If the symptom persists, have him or her stop. This is not the calming technique for that student; there are others to choose from (see the Centering Techniques box on page 118). You might offer the child a mandala or other design to color while the others are decorating their spirals.

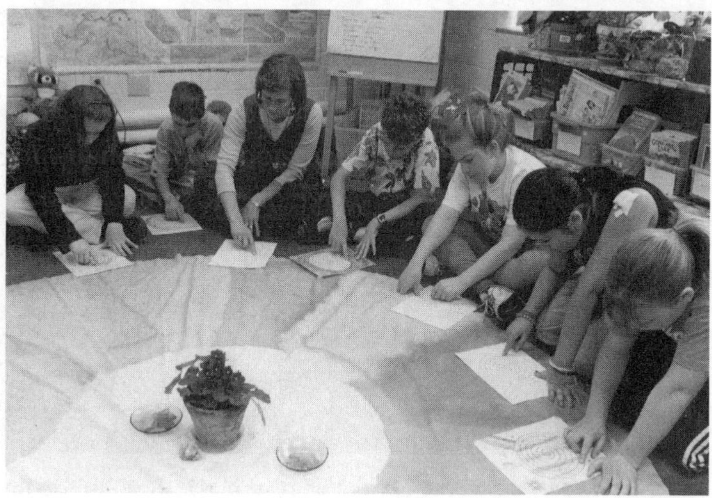

Finger-walking their spirals at the beginning of the school day helps students calm and focus themselves so they can give their full attention to their schoolwork.

Tips for Using Spirals or Labyrinths

- After they have been decorated, laminate the paper spirals for durability.
- Make reduced copies of the spiral or labyrinth so each student can put one in the corner of his or her desk for ready access.
- Have students tape their decorated spirals to the sides of their desks, so they can quickly flip them up on the desktop when needed.

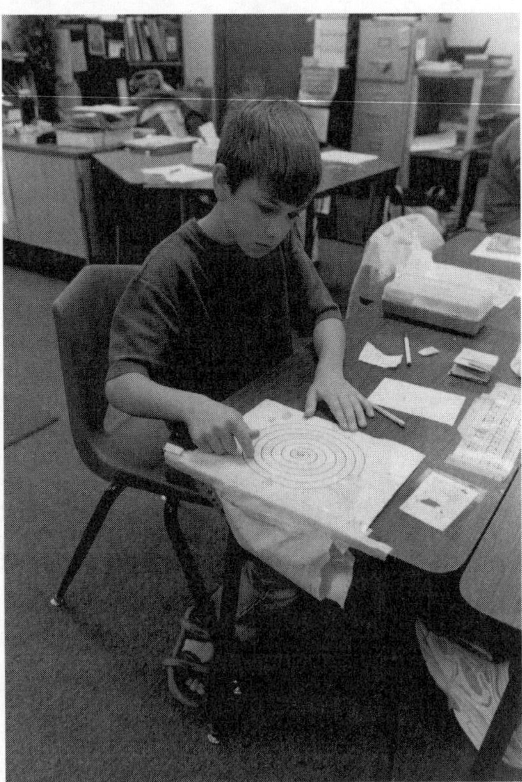

This student taped his spiral to the edge of his desk so he can flip it face-up on his desktop whenever he needs it.

- An older student who moves from room to room for classes might tape a spiral or Cretan labyrinth to the inside cover of his or her assignment book for ready access.

- It might be a good idea to have available a couple of spirals with raised lines for those students who need a more tactile approach. Depending upon the age and dexterity of your students, you may prefer to make these spirals yourself, rather than having students make them. Trace or copy a spiral onto a heavy material such as tag board or foam board. Run a line of glue all the way along the spiral line, and let it dry to form a raised line. Now a student can run an index finger between the glue guidelines to trace the spiral.
- Students will need to learn when to use the spiral or labyrinth as a tool for calming and refocusing. Cue them verbally ("How about trying your spiral, Mary?") or simply say the student's name and draw a spiral in the air for a nonverbal cue.

Affirmations

Affirmations are positive statements about how you want to be, what you want to do, or what you want to have. They can become the focus of a group centering activity or can be used with individual students when needed. Here's how to create an affirmation:

An **affirmation** is a positive statement, often beginning with either "I am" or "I have." Examples are "Math is easy for me" and "I have many friends!" The thought is phrased in **present tense,** as if it is already true. Do *not* begin an affirmation with "I will" or "I want" because if the affirmation is phrased in future tense, that is exactly where the thought will stay—in the future. It will never happen.

What we think becomes reality. If we think that we aren't good at something, we won't be. If we think that we can't make friends, we won't. Changing our negative thoughts into positive thoughts through affirmations supported by the breath makes a difference in who we become and how we operate in our lives. By breathing deeply while saying an affirmation, we create space within our bodies where the new, positive idea can live and grow. As we exhale, the old, negative idea is squeezed out with no place to live.

Creating Affirmation Strips

Objectives

- To increase students' belief in themselves and their abilities
- To help students move through emotional upsets and distractions
- To empower students to focus more fully on their work

Materials

✔ chart paper and markers
✔ 1 strip of 2" x 18" construction paper per student, in various colors
✔ dark colors of crayons or markers
✔ masking tape

1. Have your students brainstorm positive affirmations that will help them believe in themselves and their abilities or do their best work in school. Write them on chart paper for future reference. This helps students who have difficulty thinking of ideas and provides a ready reference if students want to change their affirmations later on.
2. Ask each student to select two or three affirmations and write them all on a strip of construction paper. If students have affirmation ideas that are not listed, ask them to check with you before writing them down. You want to be sure that all the affirmations are written in the now!
3. Let students tape their affirmation strips to their desks.
4. Emphasize that the effectiveness of an affirmation is tied to repeating it often and inhaling deeply as one says it, to breathe the statement in.

By repeating their affirmations, your students are reprogramming their thinking about themselves, planting the seed for change, and giving it space to grow as they fully inflate their lungs. For example, imagine that Juan has difficulty learning his multiplication facts. He might inhale deeply and repeat the affirmation, "I know my multiplication facts" every day when he arrives at school and before taking a math test. The result is that Juan begins to believe in himself, and his math performance begins to improve. What he believes becomes his reality.

> What you put your attention on grows and becomes permanent in your life. Move away from the negative, and put your attention on what it is that you really do want to be or have.
>
> —Louise L. Hay, *You Can Heal Your Life* (p. 76)

The affirmations can be changed periodically, and students can say them at home as well as at school. To make affirmations the focus of a centering session, have your students bring their attention to one of their affirmations, saying it to themselves as they breathe in. This gives the affirmation plenty of room to fill up their cells with the positive statement. The more times the affirmation is said, the sooner the change in belief or performance will occur.

I do great work every day.

I am a good friend.

Bear in mind that the effectiveness of these centering techniques will differ for each student. The elevator technique may work well for some students, whereas deep abdominal breathing will work better for others. Therefore, when you see that the class as a whole needs calming, you might offer them a menu of centering techniques to choose from. These could even be written on a list posted on a bulletin board. You might say, "I see that we all need to get more focused. You may choose to center with one of the centering techniques on the Centering Techniques list. Choose what works best for you. Let's do this for one minute (or, at first, for only 30 seconds). Get yourselves ready. Begin." When the time is up, have your students sit silently for a few seconds before resuming their work.

Centering Techniques

- doing deep abdominal breathing
- finger-walking a spiral or labyrinth
- doing a yoga pose
- holding your hands over your heart
- taking the elevator
- recalling an image from a visualization

Although this may seem counterintuitive, movement is another way to increase focus and attention. Find out how in chapter 12.

Chapter 12

Increasing Concentration through Movement

Movement can help focusing abilities? Yes indeed! Getting up and moving can definitely be beneficial for either quieting or energizing your students. The following movement activities work to harness and quiet your students' scattered energy so that they are able to refocus and get back on task.

Calming Movement Activities

In this section, I present some controlled movement activities that help to lower students' energy levels so they can focus better.

Mirroring

Because mirroring requires concentration, it is an excellent activity to help your students become more focused. Initially, have them mirror you. As they become familiar with the activity, they can do it in pairs as well, as described later. The beauty of this activity is that you can easily slip it in during transition times.

Objectives

- To promote students' concentration
- To help students refocus during transition times

Materials

✔ music with a slow tempo, such as New Age or baroque instrumentals (see Resource List)

1. Have students stand behind or next to their desks. They are to imagine that you are looking into a mirror and that they are your reflection. They are to do everything that you do.
2. Show your students the size of the mirror by outlining an area around your upper body with your hands. All movements must take place within this mirror space.
3. Turn on the music and begin to move your arms, hands, head, and face slowly and deliberately in time to the music. Remain standing in one place (remember you cannot step outside the mirror area). Remind students to reflect back to you *exactly* what they see. (Watch carefully to identify any students with directional problems. These students may need further support at a later time.)
4. Continue until you sense that your students are refocused and ready to get back to work.

Mirroring requires students to focus their attention on your movements. They can then transfer this concentration to their work.

Partner Mirroring

Partner Mirroring is an extension of Mirroring you can introduce once students are familiar with the basic procedure.

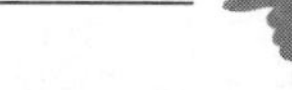

Objectives

- to promote students' concentration
- to help students refocus

Materials

- ✔ cymbal (or chime)
- ✔ music with a slow tempo, such as New Age or baroque instrumentals (see Resource List)

1. Have students pair up, and within each pair designate one partner as the viewer and the other as the reflection.
2. When the music starts, the viewer outlines the mirror and begins moving slowly and deliberately. As before, movements cannot extend beyond the mirror area, and students must remain in one place. The reflection mirrors the viewer's movements as closely as possible.
3. When you sound a chime or cymbal, students trade roles: The reflection takes over leading the movements while the viewer mirrors them.

4. As your students become proficient with this activity, have them switch roles without a cue from you. This requires deep concentration, in order to sense when it is time to switch roles. Your students might figure out a nonverbal cue they can use to switch roles.

Partner mirroring enhances students' focusing abilities as they alternate the roles of viewer and reflection.

The Blue Egg

1. Tell your students that they all have one blue egg apiece (or whatever color suits your fancy) under their desks, which will be theirs for the entire school year. They must treat it with care so that it lasts all year!
2. Ask your students to reach under their desks and gently bring out their eggs. There will probably be at least one student who will deliberately drop the egg on the floor. One way to respond is to say that the egg is magical and can repair itself

Objectives

- To increase students' concentration
- To engage students' imaginations
- To enhance students' problem-solving abilities
- To provide the basis for creative writing experiences (optional)

Materials

✔ soft, slow, flowing music (such as *The Fairy Ring,* see Resource List)

✔ cymbal (or chime)

once, but only once. That is it! There may also be one or two students who are so literal that they cannot find their blue eggs. Just go over to them and show them yours by shaping it in your hand, so they recognize that it is imaginary. You might even reach under the desk, pull out the blue egg, shape it, and place it in the child's hands.

3. Explain that students will be doing a number of activities with their eggs, in either self-space or general space. Define **self-space** as the space around them as high, wide, and low as they can reach. Define **general space** as all the open space in the classroom designated for movement.
4. Explain that you will be giving your students a series of movements to do with their eggs. When you sound the cymbal (or chime), they will start the movement. When you sound the cymbal again, they are to freeze and relax until you present the next movement experience. Instruct children through a variety of movement experiences with their eggs, such as the following:
   - tossing the egg in the air and catching it (self-space)
   - tossing the egg under an arm or a leg and catching it (self-space)
   - tossing the egg back and forth with a partner (self-space)
   - placing the egg on the palm of one hand and letting it guide you around the room to soft music (general space)
   - placing the egg on top of your head and balancing it as you walk in time to the music (general space)
   - placing the egg on some other body part and having it lead you around the room to soft music (general space)

Variations

- You can increase the problem-solving challenge by having your students do the activities at different heights (high, medium, low), in different directions (forward, backward, sideways to the left or right, diagonally to the left or right, upward or downward), and along various pathways (straight, curved, zigzag), remembering, of course, that they must not let their eggs break (Gilbert 1992). For example: "Put your egg in your dominant hand. Hold it high overhead and let it lead you around the room in a straight pathway. If you see that you might run into someone, change direction." "Now, hold your egg at medium height and let it lead you in a zigzag pathway."
- Another option is to present a new activity while the students are in motion, without sounding the chime or cymbal to freeze them.
- The blue egg is a great topic for numerous creative writing activities. Students could either collaboratively or independently write a series of "Blue Egg" stories, creating a series of recurring egg characters.

> With support, and with permission to move in the classroom in a positive manner, [the child] will unfold in his unique and complete intelligence in a way that is natural and easy. He will not be blocked; he will be free to learn.
>
> —Paul E. Dennison and Gail E. Dennison
> *Brain Gym* (p. 2)

Energizing Movement Activities

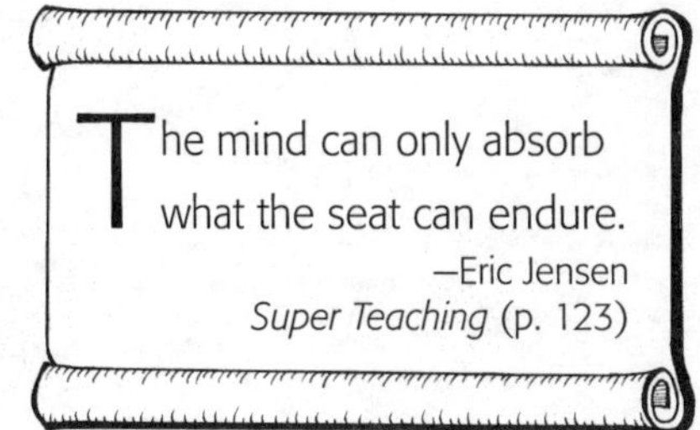

The mind can only absorb what the seat can endure.
—Eric Jensen
Super Teaching (p. 123)

There are, of course, times when students need to get up and moving, not calm down. Your students can't perform optimally unless they get oxygenated periodically. So get your class up and moving! Get their circulation going! Eric Jensen writes in *Super Teaching*, "An oxygen break every fifteen minutes is not too much" (Jensen 1995, 165).

You might be thinking, "An oxygen break every fifteen minutes! How will I ever get everything done?" Don't panic! Just watch your students and notice when their attention seems to wane. Our bodies have high and low cycles that fluctuate about every 90 to 110 minutes. Attention and learning tend to drop at the bottom of the cycle (Jensen 1998). So watch for this lull and introduce a "wake-up session" to combat it. A quick water break may provide a good opportunity for students to move. Remember that dehydration contributes to lethargy.

Move the Way You Feel

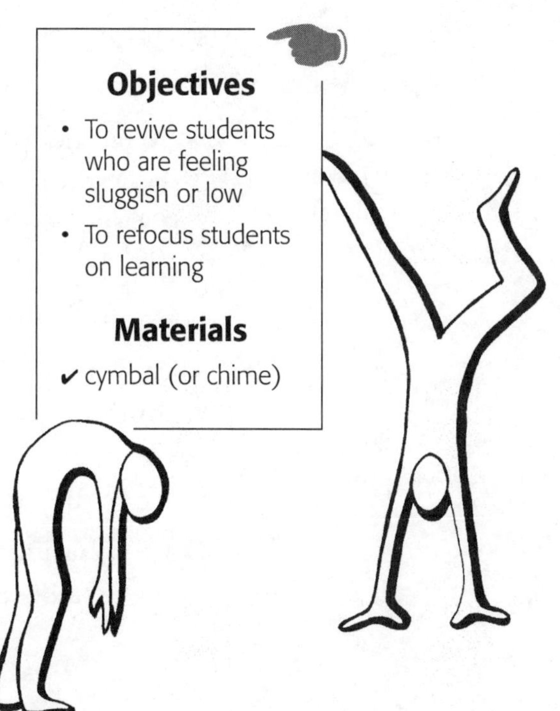

Objectives

- To revive students who are feeling sluggish or low
- To refocus students on learning

Materials

✔ cymbal (or chime)

1. Have each student find a personal self-space within the general space of the classroom. Ask each one to think of a word or a phrase that describes how he or she is feeling. Students are to think the word, not say it aloud.
2. On the sound of the cymbal (or chime), students are to move safely through the general space in a manner that shows how they are feeling. When the cymbal sounds again, they are to stop and hold that pose.

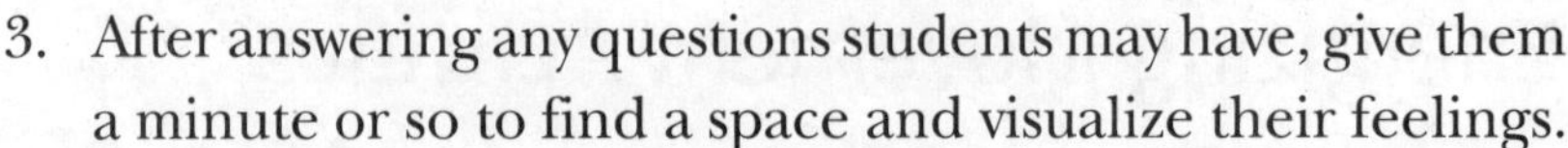

3. After answering any questions students may have, give them a minute or so to find a space and visualize their feelings.
4. Strike the cymbal and watch as your students move around the room in general space. Notice whose movements are tired and heavy. Strike the cymbal again after a few minutes. Have them freeze momentarily, then relax.
5. Lead a brief discussion about how the students moved. Here are questions you might ask:

- What showed you how your classmates were feeling?
- How did your classmates hold their bodies if they were feeling low?
- What emotions might be associated with feeling low?
- How did your classmates hold their bodies if they were feeling good?
- What emotions might be associated with feeling good?

6. Next have students move in a way that is the opposite of how they are feeling. Strike the cymbal again and watch them move through general space. After a few minutes, sound the cymbal again and ask them what they noticed this time:

- What happened when you moved the opposite of the way you felt?

7. Lead them to conclude that if they are feeling sluggish, getting up and moving in the opposite way can help them boost their spirits and feel energized again.
8. Allow your students to move (safely) in an energized way around the room for another few minutes, until the cymbal sounds again. When they hear the cymbal, they are to move in the same energized way back to their desks.
9. Close by having your students sit down at their desks and take a couple of deep belly breaths before resuming their work.

It is amazing how a change in thought combined with movement can make a difference in one's energy level. The body and mind work together to change our feelings, and thus, our state of being. This is not just for kids. Try it yourself and see what it does for you!

> The old model of education maintained that learning was a mental function separate from our bodies. Researchers now tell us how important our whole self is in the learning process. Our mood, eye patterns, and diet, for example, strongly affect learning, as do our physiology, mind state, posture, and breathing. Learning to learn better must include the awareness that the mind-body relationship is integral.
>
> —Eric Jensen, *Super Teaching* (p. 26)

Isolations

Another way to turn lethargy into energy, and to release tension as well, is with isolations. Have students do as many cycles of this exercise as you feel are needed.

Objectives

- To turn lethargy into energy
- To release students' tension
- To refocus students on their work

Materials

None

1. Have your students stand up behind or next to their desks. Explain that you will lead them in some exercises.
2. Wake up the feet and calves by having your students point the toes of one foot toward the floor, then flex the foot to point the toes upward. As the heel comes to the floor, the other foot presses into the floor for stability. Alternate pointing and flexing the toes to your cadence of "toes up,

toes down, up, down, up, down, and stop." If some students have difficulty balancing, have them hold onto the side of their desks. Repeat with the other foot.

3. To bring the hips into motion, have your students place their hands on their hips and place their feet shoulder width apart. They swing their hips to one side then the other as you say, "Right . . . left . . . right . . . left." They should swing their hips far enough to shift their weight from foot to foot. That is, as they swing to the left, the left hip rises and the right leg bends at the knee (and vice versa as they swing to the right).
4. Standing in the same position, you can have students circle their hips to the right and to the left.
5. Have students move their rib cages forward and backward several times, as you call: "Move your ribs front, back, front, back, front, back, and stop."
6. Wake up the arms. Have students begin with their arms at their sides. They push their arms from the shoulders out to the side and back, then up above the head and back, and finally down to the ground. Repeat this entire sequence as you call, "Arms out . . . and back, up . . . and back, down . . . and back, out . . . and back, up . . . and back, down . . . and back, out . . . and back, up . . . and back, down . . . and back, and stop."
7. Have students circle their wrists to the right and to the left.
8. Have students shrug both shoulders up and down, then alternate the right shoulder up and down, then the left shoulder up and down. Say, "Up, down, up, down, and stop" or "Right, left, right, left, and stop."
9. You can also have students roll their shoulders forward and backward, either both together or one after the other, like this: "Right forward, left forward, right forward, left forward, and stop," or "Right backward, left backward, right backward, left backward, and stop."

10. Instruct your students to turn their heads from side to side, slowly and only as far as feels comfortable (so they don't hyperextend their necks). Say, "Right, middle, left, middle, right, middle, left, middle, right, middle, and stop."
11. Repeat the same series with looking up, straight ahead, and down, as you call, "Up, center, down, center, up, center, and stop." (Remind students to move their heads gently only as far as is comfortable and, when looking up, to curve their necks slightly in a *C* shape.)

Moving to the Beat of a Percussion Instrument

Another quick and fun way to energize your students is to get them moving to the beat of a percussion instrument.

Objectives

- To energize students
- To help students refocus on their work
- To elevate the mood of the class

Materials

✔ some type of percussion instrument (I like to use a cymbal or Native American drum.)

1. Have your students stand next to their desks. Explain that they will be moving to the beat of a drum in general space. They have to follow the beat. That means if the beat is fast, they move quickly, and if the beat is slow, they move slowly.
2. Say, "When I say so and not before, move to the beat of the drum in general space. Remember that you must move safely. When the drum stops, you must freeze where you are."
3. Begin beating the drum and watch your students as they move, one step per beat. You might want to move with them.

4. You may wish to vary the tempo of the drumbeats while your students are moving. This requires that they listen intently for the change to stay in step.
5. When you are ready to conclude, have your students move back to their seats with the drumbeats. Have them take a couple of deep abdominal breaths before sitting down and going back to work.

You may well be boosting your students' energy levels without realizing it. Interactive activities that get your students out of their seats and moving around the classroom are energy boosting. Examples are rotating between work stations and surveying different classrooms for a math project. Teaching curricular concepts through movement is another way to get the circulation going (for example, having pairs of students demonstrate parallel and perpendicular lines). You can easily build these energy-boosting activities into your teaching, rather than planning specific movement activities. Combine interactive activities with periodic wake-me-uppers, and you'll see positive results.

Movement for relaxation or energizing helps your students focus their attention where it needs to be. And while it's helping them, it's helping you as well, if you join in. The sound of music can do the same thing, as we'll see in the next chapter.

Chapter 13

Using Music

Oh, the sound of music! It can make you feel calm and quiet inside, as if you are floating among the clouds. It can make you feel joyful and want to dance about. There is a duality in the power of music, a yin and a yang side. The yin is soft, soothing, and nurturing. The yang is vibrant, energizing, and active. You can take advantage of the dual nature of music to help your students reach a positive state for learning and doing their best work. Of course, you will benefit too.

The Yin and Yang of Music

Yin music is instrumental, has a relatively slow tempo, and is soft and soothing, promoting slow, deep breathing. The mind quiets and calms, stress melts away, encouraging relaxation and improved attention. Campbell (1997) lists several benefits of music. It can

- reduce stress and tension
- calm the mind
- relieve anxiety
- relax the body

It is music with these characteristics that I am referring to as yin music.

Yang music has a relatively fast tempo with a strong beat that increases heart rate. The body becomes energized and the mind more alert. This type of music is usually instrumental, but vocal pieces may be used during transition times. According to Campbell (1997), music has other benefits as well. It can

- activate
- energize
- motivate

Music with these characteristics is what I am calling yang music.

Selecting Appropriate Music

Once again, pay attention to the emotional temperatures and energy levels of your students when choosing music. Are they restless, lethargic, distracted, or overly energetic? Do they need relaxing or energizing? What kind of music will create the desired result? In his book *The Mozart Effect,* Don Campbell (1997, 78–79) suggests various types of music, which I have divided into yin and yang categories:

Yin Music

- classical: Mozart, Haydn
- baroque (slower works)
- Gregorian chants
- New Age

Yang Music

- jazz (lively), Dixieland, reggae
- marches
- *The Macarena*
- movie themes

It is wise to listen to your musical selection in advance to make sure that you like it and that the lyrics, if any, are appropriate for your students. Ask yourself the following questions:

 *What selections do I enjoy?*

 *Which selections have appropriate lyrics?*

Try out these pieces with your students to get a sense of what appeals to them. Refine your selections based on their responses by asking yourself:

 *What selections do my students enjoy?*

 *What effect do these selections have on my students?*

Have a selection of three or four of both types of music available for variety. You may wish to use labels or different colored stickers to code your tapes or compact disks as yin or yang for quick selection. You also might want to make a yang tape of pop tunes by several artists that have age-appropriate lyrics for your students. Specific tapes and compact disks that I enjoy using can be found in the Resource List.

You can use yin music for relaxation with individual students as well as with the entire class. You could allow a particular student who needs calming to sit in a private work space and listen to music through headphones for several minutes. Give the student a one- or three-minute timer and instructions to return to his or her desk when the allotted time is up. Alternatively, during independent work periods, the student could remain in the work space and complete his or her work while listening to music.

If you introduce the use of the headset early in the year as a calming option, you should have few problems with other students complaining, "When do I get a turn to use the headset?" or "How come I don't get to use the headset?" Your students will understand that this is a calming tool used when needed with those for whom it is effective. If you have a listening center with headsets in your classroom, you can remind your students that they all get to use a headset sometimes, but for a different reason. Another way to use yin music to enhance the learning environment is by playing quiet background music with a tempo of 60 beats per minute for the whole class to listen to during silent reading or seat work. Selections of this type, common in some styles of baroque and New Age music, improve alertness and state of being for more focused learning (Campbell 1997).

The duality of music, the yin and the yang, can go a long way in helping your students do their best work. It is a powerful and pleasurable technique well worth remembering and implementing.

And Now for the Fortune Cookie

You've sampled each dish on the pu pu platter, tasted it, chewed it, savored it. You know what you like and what feng shui adjustments help to create a nurturing and supportive classroom environment. You know what techniques bring relaxation or increase energy so that optimum teaching and learning can take place. That's great. But you can't leave a Chinese restaurant without having a fortune cookie!

The fortune cookie holds the invisible benefit of using the techniques you've chosen. What is this benefit? It is empowerment: empowerment of the classroom space, empowerment of yourself, and empowerment of your students. This empowerment comes from the heart: from your love for yourself, your love for your students, and your love for teaching and learning. By nurturing and supporting your own and your students' well-being, you empower everyone in the classroom community to create a better teaching and learning experience for themselves. You're on your way to creating a peaceable classroom community and a more peaceful world. Ta da!

Resource List

Meditation Aids

Benedictine Monks of Santo Domingo de Silos. *Chant.* Angel Records CDC72435, 1994 [compact disk].

Kabat-Zinn, Jon. *Mindfulness Meditation Practice Tapes.* Stress Reduction Tapes S2-1, S2-2, S2-3, S2-4, and S2-5 [audiotapes]. Available from Stress Reduction Tapes, P.O. Box 547, Lexington, MA 02420. www.mindfulnesstapes.com.

Tashi, Ven. Karma. *Meditation Music: Tibetan Singing Bowls.* Tibetan Music Center, Nepal, TMC 1002, 1999 [compact disk].

Yin Music

Campbell, Don. *The Mozart Effect Music for Children,* vol. 2, *Relax, Daydream and Draw.* Children's Group 84292-2, 1997 [compact disk]. Available from Children's Group, 1400 Bayly Street, Suite 7, Pickering, Ont. Canada L1W 3R2. (800) 757-8372. www.childrensgroup.com.

Markoe, Gerald Jay. *The Pleiades.* Astro Music 027, 1997 [compact disk]. Available from Audio Alternatives, P.O. Box 405, Chappaqua, NY 10514.

Pachelbel Canon with Ocean Sounds. Real Music RM 5554 [compact disk]. Available from Real Music, 85 Libertyship Way, Suite 207, Sausalito, CA 94965.

Pickens, Harry. 2002. *Peace and Quiet: Calm Your Classroom.* San Diego, Calif: Brain Store. Available from the Brain Store, 4202 Sorrento Valley Blvd., Ste. B, San Diego, CA 92121. Phone: (800) 325-4769, FAX: 858-546-7560. www.thebrainstore.com/store.

Relax with the Classics, vol. 1: *Largo.* Lind Institute LI-501, 1987 [audiotape]. Available from Lind Institute, P.O. Box 14487, San Francisco, CA 94114. (800) 462-3766.

Rowland, Mike. *The Fairy Ring.* Enso Records ND-62801, 1995 [compact disk]. Available from Enso Records, P.O. Box 17662, Glendale, WI 53217-0662.

John, Werner. *The Healing Flute: Native American Flute Solos.* Early Light Music EL3312, 2000 [compact disk]. Available from Early Light Music, P.O. Box 233, Hadley, MA 01035, (800) 356-0987, www.woodflutes.com.

Yang Music

Campbell, Don. *The Mozart Effect: Music for Children,* vol. 3: *Mozart in Motion.* Children's Group 84293-2, 1997 [compact disk]. Available from Children's Group, 1400 Bayly Street, Suite 7, Pickering, Ont. Canada L1W 3R2. (800) 757-8372. www.childrensgroup.com.

Higby, Scott, and Eric Jensen, producers. 2002. *Adrenaline to Go!: Getting Things Done!* San Diego, Calif: Brain Store. Available from the Brain Store, 4202 Sorrento Valley Blvd., Ste. B, San Diego, CA 92121. Phone: (800) 325-4769, FAX: 858-546-7560. www.thebrainstore.com/store.

Joplin, Scott. *Greatest Hits.* RCA Victor 60842-4-RG, 1991 [audiotape].

Macarena Club Cutz. RCA Victor 66745-2, 1996 (also available from BMG Music) [compact disk].

Sousa, John Philip. *Sousa Marches.* Band of the Grenadier Guards, Major Rodney Bashford, Polygram 448 957-2, 1996 [compact disk].

Spiral Rock Art

Hirschmann, Fred. 1994. *Rock Art of the American Southwest.* Portland, Ore.: Graphic Arts Center Publications. (This coffee table book contains beautiful color photographs of rock art.)

Malotki, Ekkehart. 2000. *Kokopelli: The Making of an Icon.* Lincoln: University of Nebraska Press. (Although this book focuses on the flute player, Kokopelli, much of the rock art in the photos includes spirals.)

Zephyr Press Resources

Brewer, Chris, and Don Campbell. 1991. *Rhythms of Learning: Creative Tools for Developing Lifelong Skills.* Tucson, Ariz.: Zephyr Press.

Kaufeldt, Martha. 1999. *Begin with the Brain: Orchestrating the Learner Centered Classroom.* Tucson, Ariz.: Zephyr Press.

Reference List

Barnett, Libby, and Maggie Chambers, with Susan Davidson. 1996. *Reiki Energy Medicine: Bringing Healing Touch into Home, Hospital, and Hospice.* Rochester, Vt.: Healing Arts Press.

Burmeister, Alice, with Tom Monte. 1997. *The Touch of Healing: Energizing the Body, Mind, and Spirit with the Art of Jin Shin Jyutsu.* New York: Bantam Books.

Campbell, Don. 1997. *The Mozart Effect: Tapping the Power of Music to Heal the Body, Strengthen the Mind, and Unlock the Creative Spirit.* New York: Avon Books.

————. 2000. *The Mozart Effect for Children: Awakening Your Child's Mind, Health, and Creativity with Music.* New York: HarperCollins.

Dennison, Paul E., and Gail E. Dennison. 1994. *Brain Gym: Teacher's Edition.* Rev. ed. Ventura, Calif.: Edu-Kinesthetics.

Ellis, Richard. 1999. *Practical Reiki.* New York: Sterling Publishing.

Frey, Susan. 1999. *The Road to Avalon II: Cultivating Spirituality in the Classroom.* Haverford, Pa.: Infinity Publishing.

Gilbert, Anne Green. 1992. *Creative Dance for All Ages.* Reston, Va.: American Alliance for Health, Physical Education, Recreation, and Dance.

Hannaford, Carla. 1995. *Smart Moves: Why Learning Is Not All in Your Head.* Arlington, Va.: Great Ocean Publishers.

Hay, Louise L. 1987. *You Can Heal Your Life.* Carlsbad, Calif.: Hay House.

Hendricks, Gay. 1995. *Conscious Breathing: Breathwork for Health, Stress Relief, and Personal Mastery.* New York: Bantam Books.

Jensen, Eric. 1995. *Super Teaching.* San Diego, Calif.: Brain Store.

————. 1998. *Introduction to Brain Compatible Learning.* San Diego, Calif.: Brain Store.

Kabat-Zinn, Jon. 1994. *Wherever You Go There You Are: Mindfulness Meditation for Everyday Life.* New York: Hyperion.

Kent, Howard. 1999. *The Complete Illustrated Guide to Yoga: A Practical Approach to Achieving Optimum Health for Mind, Body, and Spirit.* Boston, Mass.: Element Books.

Khalsa, Gurucharan Singh, and Yogi Bhajan. 2000. *Breathwalk: Breathing Your Way to a Revitalized Body, Mind, and Spirit.* New York: Broadway Books.

Krucoff, Carol. 2000. "Inhale, Exhale—What's So Hard about It?" *Nashua (New Hampshire) Telegraph,* July 16.

Lusk, Julie T. 1998. *Desktop Yoga.* New York: Penguin Putnam.

Rutt, Stephanie. n.d. *Breathe: The Breath as Teacher: Diaphragmatic Breathing.* Milford, N.H.: Author.

Sarley, Dinabandhu, and Ila Sarley. 1999. *The Essentials of Yoga.* New York: Random House.

"Technique Gives Students a Breather." 2001. *The Charlotte Sun (Port Charlotte, Fla.),* December 16.

Weil, Andrew. 1997. *Eight Weeks to Optimum Health: A Program for Taking Full Advantage of Your Body's Natural Healing Power.* New York: Alfred A. Knopf.

West, Melissa Gayle. 2000. *Exploring the Labyrinth: A Guide for Healing and Spiritual Growth.* New York: Random House.

Wydra, Nancilee. 1996. *Feng Shui: The Book of Cures: 150 Simple Solutions for Health and Happiness in Your Home or Office.* Chicago: Contemporary Books.

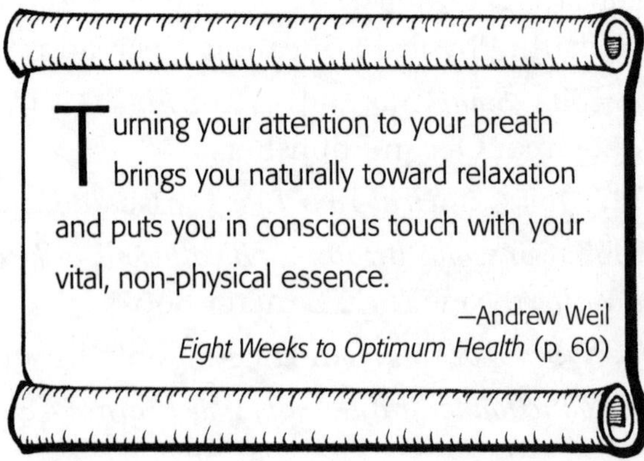

About the Author

Sandy Bothmer received her B.S. in education from Northern Illinois University and her M.Ed. from Lesley University. She has 21 years of teaching experience with students ranging from preschool through grade five, in addition to teaching a writers' workshop for a Gifted and Talented program. Currently, Sandy works as an educational consultant and workshop presenter, as well as teaching a creative yoga and movement class for children in Amherst, New Hampshire. A certified Reiki Master, Intuitive Healer, and Magnified Healing Instructor, Sandy also has a private practice in the field of energy medicine.

Index

O–P

R

S

T

V–W

Y